The Third Reich

Adolf Hitler, Nazi Germany, World War II and The Last German Empire

By Frank D. Kennedy

Table of Contents

Introduction

What was the Third Reich?

The Third Reich was one of the names given to Germany from 1933-1945, the period during which it was controlled by the Nazi party under the leadership of Adolf Hitler. But what is a *reich*? And why was Hitler's reich the third one?

A brief etymology of the word *reich*

A peculiar thing began to happen at the end of the second World War, after Hitler was defeated and the atrocities of the Holocaust had come to light. All things that were German became tainted with Nazism, while *Nazi* itself became cultural shorthand for *evil*. Unfair though this may have been to some Germans, the language and the accent took on a sinister symbolic value across the western world. People with German-sounding names often changed their spelling or pronunciation to avoid hostility or uncomfortable tensions. An American woman once told the story of an angry coworker who insisted that it was indecent of her not to have abandoned the Germanic surname she was born with. This woman's distant ancestors were indeed German, but her family had been living in America since the 19th century. The name her family had bestowed on her seemed particularly redolent of Nazism to her hostile colleague: it was *Reich.*

There is a popular conception amongst English speakers that the word *reich* was coined by the Nazis, or else that it means something sinister, but this isn't the case. *Reich* is simply the German word for "realm". *Konigreich,* or "king's realm", is the equivalent of the English word "kingdom"; *kaiserreich* is the word that means "empire", or rather, "realm of the emperor." It is no more inherently Nazi than any other word in the German language which happened to be commonly used in political discourse.

Interestingly, the title born by the German emperors, *kaiser,* is related to the word *caesar*—as in *Caesar Augustus* or *Tiberius Caesar.* This is not a coincidence. German rulers have perceived their domain as being the legitimate successor to the ancient Roman Empire since the time of Charlemagne.

Every country has their national myth. In the United States, the American Dream has enchanted millions by promising wealth and prosperity to anyone willing to work hard and seize the right opportunities. In Germany, from the time of the Carolingian kings in the 8th century until the defeat of the Nazis in 1945, the dream had been that of a vast empire, united under one strong leader, who would usher his people to glory by recreating the triumphs of the greatest civilizations in human history.

Das Dritte Reich

"The political situation is so delicate that it must be handled with the utmost care and skill. We cannot yet be sure that we are not heading for national annihilation. We shall certainly perish as a European people—and Europe will perish with us—unless we learn to utilize, with a political wisdom learnt from our revolutionary experiences, the possibilities that still lie open before us."

Arthur Moeller van den Bruck, *Das Dritte Reich*

The English translation of *Das Dritte Reich* is called *Germany's Third Empire*, but it is also referred to as *The Third Reich.* In the early days of the Nazi movement, this book played a formative role in shaping the ideology of party leaders. And it is probably responsible for the fact that we still speak of Nazi Germany as the Third Reich today.

Germany after the end of the first World War was a country humiliated, not only by its military defeat, but by the punishing reparations dictated by the Treaty of Versailles. The German economy collapsed, and the German people were seeking to re-establish their sense of a proud national identity. This was the political climate in which *Das Dritte Reich* was published in 1923. Van der Bruck's book made painful yet not inaccurate reference to the fact that Germans of the post-war generation felt adrift and lacking in pride and purpose. Not since the Second

German Empire, or Second Reich, during which Germany was united by Otto von Bismarck under the Kaisers, had Germans felt the sort of nationalistic pride they would later be stirred to under Hitler.

Years before Hitler and the Nazi party came to power, van der Bruck theorized that a Third Reich would be founded by a generation which had rejected the crippling strictures of the Treaty of Versailles. Above all, he emphasized the need for a strong central leader. As van der Bruck was an admirer of Benito Mussolini and Italian fascism, the strong leader he had in mind shared many of Mussolini's qualities—namely, the authority to make decisions on behalf of his country without reference to a parliament or other democratic processes. In short, van der Bruck felt that Germany needed a dictator. In 1923, dictators were not yet feared and despised in quite the same way they are now. For awhile, Mussolini and Hitler were widely admired in Europe, even in countries such as England and the United States, before the full extent of their crimes and abuses began to come to light. They were seen as men of strength and vision, possessing the authority of monarchs, but rising to power by virtue of their own talents and charisma.

Hitler's Germany

When we hear of the Third Reich, we are not immediately given to wonder about the German empires that came before it, or to ponder the reasons why visions of empire-building were so particularly appealing to the German people in the aftermath of the first World War. Instead, we think immediately of Hitler, of Nazi flags, the invasion of Poland, bombs falling on London, and the Holocaust. That is what the Third Reich will always be to us, and accordingly, a third of this book is dedicated to explaining how Hitler's regime operated in Germany during the twelve years the Nazis held power.

But as this book is aimed at the layperson whose knowledge of German history is general rather than specialist in nature, it attempts to expand on the traditional narrative that most people have derived from high school social studies lessons, the occasional documentary film, and popular culture. It accounts for the rise of the Third Reich by placing Adolf Hitler, the rise of Nazism, and the goals of fascist Germany, into a historical and cultural context such as the reader may not have been exposed to before.

In her 1964 memoir, entitled *Fazit,* or *Account Rendered,* former Nazi Melita Maschman describes the mindset she had as a very young girl who grew up during Hitler's rise to power. She writes:

"Before I understood the meaning of the word 'Germany,' I loved it as something mysteriously overshadowed with grief…"

Those of us who grew up in the western world in the generations after the second World War may not fully appreciate the vulnerabilities in the German consciousness which were created by the poverty and shame that followed their defeat in the first World War. We may not consider, without prompting, how those vulnerabilities were exploited by the Nazis during their rise to power. American readers in particular may have never been in position to sympathize with a people who felt that the most glorious days of their civilization lay in the distant past, and that their future held little hope for prosperity, stability, or greatness.

The bulk of this book will be dedicated to a study of how the Nazis came to power and how the second World War erupted as a consequence. However, in order to understand the social and political conditions that gave birth to Nazi ideology and which enabled it to hold sway over the country for twelve years, we will spend two chapters examining the state of Germany after the end of World War I, an era spanning from the abdication of the Kaiser in 1918 to the fall of the Weimar Republic in 1933.

And before we embark on a study of Germany in the early 20th century, Chapter One will take us back even further: first to the late middle ages and the thousand year dominion of the Holy Roman Empire, then to the mid 19th century, the Napoleonic wars, and the unification of Germany under the leadership of Otto von Bismarck.

While there is not space in a book this size for more than a brief outline of either of these subjects, such an outline will function usefully as a sketch of German history during the centuries preceding the Nazi regime. With these references to hand, the reader will be better equipped to understand why the Nazis considered themselves the heirs of history and the restorers of Germany's lost empires, and more fully appreciate the circumstances that allowed Adolf Hitler to create the Third Reich and commit atrocities in the name of the German people.

Chapter One: The First Reich and the Second Reich

The First Reich: The Founding of the Holy Roman Empire

Although the Holy Roman Empire was established under the rule of the Franks, who were ancestral forerunners of the Germans in the centuries before Germany existed as a nation, the Empire itself as a geopolitical entity comprised most of western and central Europe, encompassing such modern territories as the Czech Republic and Italy.

Like the ancient Roman Empire before it, the Holy Roman Empire did not demand that those under its rule adhere to a single imperial identity; only uniformity of religion was required. The constituent nations retained their languages and ethnic identities, and the Holy Roman Emperor was considered the king of his own nation, distinct from his Imperial office. In other words, the title of Holy Roman Emperor was not, theoretically, seated with any

13

particular nation or people; rather, it was the political and military arm of the Catholic Church, and therefore under the authority of the Pope, with the Emperor functioning as the Pope's protector and enforcer.

In the late middle ages (and for hundreds of years afterwards), the Pope was not merely the spiritual head of the Roman Catholic church, but also a temporal ruler who wielded enormous political influence. But his armies tended to be small, unable to fend off invaders encroaching on Church lands. In the late 8th century, the Church under Pope Zachary became heavily reliant for military support upon the most powerful European king of the time: Pepin III, King of the Franks, father of Charlemagne. As a direct result of this dependency, which only grew over time, Charlemagne (also known as Charles the Great) was crowned "Emperor of the Romans" by Pope Leo III in the year 800. (Most scholars refer to Charlemagne as the first Holy Roman Emperor, though the title as such was not coined until the early 10th century under the reign of Otto I.)

Charlemagne conquered most of Europe in his lifetime, and had reached the peak of his power in 800; he had been a serious and faithful supporter of the Church under the Popes before Leo, but his military might was such that he could almost certainly have deposed the Pope had he wished to. (Charlemagne's successor would, in fact, replace the Pope with a candidate for the office that was more to his liking in the next century.) The creation of the office of Holy Roman Emperor was seen as an attempt by the Pope to secure Charlemagne's loyalty to the Church with even tighter bonds than already existed, lest he be tempted to challenge Leo where he was weak.

Since the Holy Roman Emperor's authority was technically issued from the Church, it was meant to be passed down by elections, rather than bestowed by fathers on their sons at death. But the attitude of Charlemagne's immediate successors was that the Church, in granting the Imperial title to Charlemagne, had been recognizing his authority rather than granting authority of its own; that is to say, the Holy

Roman Emperor had been, and ought to be, the king of whichever constituent nation of the Empire wielded the most power, if the Church expected the Emperor to protect it. Thus, for most of the next millennium, the Frankish kings and their descendants preserved the Imperial title within their own bloodline by holding the election for their successor before their deaths, so as to ensure that the title passed to their sons.

The belief of Charlemagne and his descendants that they could trace the line of their empire from the time of the ancient Romans would be inherited by the Nazis in later centuries. Charlemagne in particular saw his own kingdom as the heir to Roman greatness, and attempted to foster the same iron rule, uniform justice, and flourishing of culture in the Frankish empire that the Pax Romana had once enabled in lands under Roman dominion. Hitler's goals were essentially the same; the Nazi program of establishing racial purity through genocide is in some ways merely the 20th century analogue of Charlemagne's campaigns to convert Europe to Christianity at sword point. But while successive generations have steadily endeavored to erase every lingering effect of Nazism from the face of the historical record, Charlemagne was rather more successful in establishing his legacy. While Charlemagne's own dynasty, that of the Carolingian kings, lasted only about one hundred years after his death, the Holy Roman Empire endured for the next thousand years.

After Charlemagne

At the end of the 9th century, the choice of which monarch was crowned Holy Roman Emperor reverted to the Pope, and thus for a few decades the Imperial crown was passed from one Italian noble to another. But by the middle of the 10th century, power had reverted back to the German kings. In 936, Otto I, also known as Otto the Great, claimed the Imperial title from the Church and established what would become known as the Ottonian Empire. For the next hundred years the Holy Roman Emperor was the supreme authority in Europe, more powerful than the Pope and no longer maintaining even a fiction of bowing to the Church's authority. The Papacy recovered its supremacy within a few decades, but the German dynasties kept the Imperial title until the dissolution of the Holy Roman Empire in 1806.

We cannot possibly cover the next nine hundred years of European history in any detail in this chapter, and there is no need to try. Our goal is simply to gain an understanding of how Hitler and the Nazis viewed German history, and the Imperial legacy they were upholding. In their own eyes, the Nazis were the legitimate successors of kings and emperors who made sweeping conquests that unified Europe as nothing had unified it since the time of ancient Romans. You can see evidence of this perceived continuity between the Third Reich and ancient Rome in Nazi regalia: the *Reichsadler,* the Imperial eagle, which appeared on the banners of the Holy Roman Empire, was also found in the coats of arms of the Second German Empire, the Weimar Republic, and Nazi Germany, where it appears clutching a wreathe surrounding a swastika. The eagle was famously the symbol of ancient Rome, and the *Bundesadler*, or federal eagle, is the symbol of the Federal Republic of Germany in the present day.

The rulers of the Ottonian, Salier, Hohenstaufen, and Habsburger dynasties spanned the nine centuries between the founding of the Holy Roman Empire and its dissolution in 1806, during the Napoleonic Wars. French forces, under self-proclaimed Emperor Napoleon Bonaparte, defeated the coalition forces supporting Franz II at the Battle of Austerlitz, and from 1812 to 1815, the German state under Napoleon was organized under the title the Coalition of the Rhine. (Napoleon abdicated in 1814, but would rally another campaign in 1815, only to be finally defeated by the English at the Battle of Waterloo after one hundred days.) After Napoleon was defeated, the German Confederation was formed at the Congress of Vienna, which united thirty nine autonomous German speaking states into a loose alliance, primarily for economic purposes. The German Confederation was a weak alliance, and it would be reorganized under different names and shifting boundary lines until the unification of Germany and the establishment of the

Hohenzollern dynasty in 1871, which endured until the abdication of Kaiser Wilhelm II in 1918.

Germany being composed of so many independent states for so much of its history sets it apart from other European nations. During the Renaissance, other European nations began to concentrate power under central monarchies, producing the modern nation state. But during the Holy Roman Empire, Germany was composed of the *Kleinstaaterei*—a semi-feudal confederation of some 300 independent German duchies, bishoprics, principalities, and Imperial Free Cities, all of which were governed independently by their own dukes, princes, bishops, and mayors, while recognizing, to differing extents, the supreme authority of the Holy Roman Emperor. The *Kleinstaaterei* were confusingly and irrationally organized. Some were no more than a single large city, while others were composed of non-contiguous territories—that is, two separate tracts of land which were separated geographically, but which were ruled by one family that had united them through royal marriages. Most but not all territories of the

Kleinstaaterei were German speaking, and after the Protestant Reformation in the 15th and 16th centuries, there was no uniformity of religion. Under the Coalition of the Rhine, Napoleon attempted to consolidate the German territories into logical, controllable entities that could be more easily governed but were neither large nor powerful enough to challenge France. This reduced their number from three hundred to about thirty, but the Coalition of the Rhine ended with Napoleon's defeat.

The political shifts in Germany during the mid to late 19th century were influenced primarily by what is known as German dualism—that is, the historical rivalry between the Kingdom of Prussia, one of the largest German states, and the Kingdom of Austria, which was German speaking, but largely Catholic, where Prussia was primarily Lutheran. Prussia and Austria had cooperated during the Napoleonic Wars, but the alliance was short lived. Both Prussia and Austria felt it had the best right to be considered the seat of German culture and influence.

Otto von Bismarck, one of the greatest diplomats in European history and a Prussian nobleman, would achieve the unification of the German states, excluding Austria, in the late 19th century under the rule of the Kaisers—the Hohenzollern dynasty, which would rule until the end of the first World War.

The Second Reich: A New German Empire

The following quote is from Bismarck's address to the lower house of the Prussian parliament, September 29, 1862.

"The position of Prussia in Germany will not be determined by its liberalism but by its power [...] Prussia must concentrate its strength and hold it for the favorable moment, which has already come and gone several times. Since the treaties of Vienna, our frontiers have been ill-designed for a healthy body politic. Not through speeches and majority decisions will the great questions of the day be decided—that was the great mistake of 1848 and 1849—but by iron and blood."

The unification of Germany and the establishment of the Hohenzollern dynasty came about in 1871, following a series of deliberate military and political maneuvers devised by Otto von Bismarck.

The Austro-Prussian War

Bismarck was appointed Foreign Minister under King Wilhelm I of Prussia in 1862, for the specific task of solving Wilhelm's irreconcilable conflict with the Prussian Diet, or parliamentary body, which refused to fund the massive increase in the army that Wilhelm wanted. Under Bismarck's guidance, Wilhelm dissolved the Diet, an unpopular move that resulted in calls for Bismarck's dismissal, which the King ignored. In 1866, seeking to retake German speaking territories which had been seized from Denmark and divided between Prussia and Austria a few years earlier, Prussia declared war on Austria. The conflict, known as the Seven Week's war or the Austro-Prussian war, was won by the Prussians at the Battle of Koniggratz. (Interestingly, the short duration of the Seven Week's War led to its being referred to as a *blitzkrieg,* or lightning war—a term adopted by the Nazis in 1939 to refer to rapid bombing attacks.)

As a result of this victory over Austria, Prussia annexed the territories of Schleswig and Holstein (the territories which had previously been under Danish rule) as well as Frankfurt, Hanover, Hesse-Kassel, and Nassau. These territories formed the North German Confederation, replacing the German Confederation, which had been formed after Napoleon's defeat. The acquisition of as many German states as possible had been Bismarck's plan since the beginning, but further conquest would require another war—and not merely an expansionist war, but a popular war that had the support of the Prussian people and the backing of the Diet, which would be responsible for funding it.

The German states, in their divided, semi-autonomous condition, were vulnerable to outside conquest, a fact which had been made plain during the Napoleonic Wars at the beginning of the 19th century. It was, in fact, the anti-French sentiment which had been created during this period that would provide

Bismarck with the justification he required to go to war again in 1870.

The Franco-Prussian War

Owing to a revolution which had taken place earlier in the decade, the throne of Spain was vacant, and in 1870 the Spanish offered it to a German prince, Leopold of Hohenzollern. The possibility of a Spanish king who would be sympathetic to the German powers greatly alarmed the French, and they demanded that Leopold refuse the throne, which he agreed to do. But Bismarck, seeking to inspire a new surge of German nationalism and hatred for the French, published in German newspapers a highly edited version of the letter in which the Spanish had demanded Leopold's demurral.

The published text, known as the Ems Dispatch, made the French sound as if they had a perfect right to meddle in German affairs of state; it was published alongside the official response of the German government, which was calculated to foster a sense of insult. None of the European nations were especially pleased with France during this era of history, owing to Napoleon's wars, and the Ems Dispatch fostered a wave of anti-French feeling across the continent. The French, resenting the way Bismarck had manipulated their words to create this effect, became just as eager for a war with Prussia as Bismarck was eager for a war with them.

On July 19, 1870, France, under Napoleon III, nephew of the emperor who had waged the Napoleonic Wars, declared war against Prussia. Napoleon was conscious of the fact that his rule would be endangered by a defeat, and had only undertaken the war with the assurance of his ministers that his army was ready to conquer the Prussians. But Bismarck had been preparing carefully and methodically for this conflict since the end of the Seven Weeks' War, and as a result the Prussian army was a miracle of efficient organization. Not only were the French defeated in January of 1871—the Prussians would occupy France for the next three years. A revolution, led by Republican (anti-monarchist) factions had erupted in Paris during the war, and the confusion in the city was such that the French and Prussian forces had to cooperate in order to defeat the revolutionaries, before the French could officially surrender.

In the Palace of Versailles, Wilhelm I was pronounced Kaiser of the German Empire. Since the late 18th century, Austria and Prussia had competed to be recognized as the power which was most capable of defending the German states, but the war against France had made it apparent that Prussia's military might was unparalleled.

Various leaders had attempted to unite Germany into a single nation-state for most of the second half of the 19th century, and under Bismarck's guidance, it had finally been accomplished. The duchies, grand-duchies, principalities, and free cities of Germany had thrown their armies behind Prussia to defeat the Germans, and now all of them, including the Catholic states in the south, were prepared to accept Prussia's leadership. The final annexations of German territories, including the French-German territory of

Alsace-Lorraine, newly surrendered by the French, were formalized by treaty in 1871.

Ironically, the treaty which created the Second German Reich was known as the Treaty of Versailles of 1871. The year is added to distinguish it from the Treaty of Versailles, which, after Germany's defeat at the end of the First World War, dissolved the Second German Empire, and by imposing astronomical reparations, created conditions of political and social unrest which would pave the way for the rise of the Nazis and the Third Reich under Adolf Hitler.

Bismarck and Balance of Power Statesmanship

In 1871, when Kaiser Wilhelm I was declared emperor of the German Empire, Otto von Bismarck was made a prince and named Chancellor of Germany. For the next nineteen years, he would devote himself to building alliances between the "Great Powers"—that is, the strongest nations on the continent—in order to maintain diplomatic balance and avoid future wars in Europe.

Scholars of the Second Reich are fairly united in the opinion that Bismarck had little desire to expand Germany's borders further, now that the consolidation of German territories had been achieved. With Germany at last unified, Bismarck's principle concern was to foster economic development within the empire, something that could only happen in conditions of peace, with good relationships between potential trading partners who were also at peace with their own neighbors. War, after all, drives prices up.

Bismarck had specific goals behind the diplomatic approach he took with each particular country. France, for instance: despite the fact that France and Germany had been at war with one another for the better part of the 19th century, and even though Bismarck had unquestionably courted, even instigated, the Franco-Prussian War, it no longer served his interests to have any conflict with France, and therefore he made every effort to maintain cordial relations between them.

At the same time, there was a strong desire for vengeance against Germany amongst the French people, after the Prussian invasion and occupation of Paris, and the imposition of heavy reparations payments, and Bismarck was well aware of this. Relations with France were so tense for a time that many German newspapers predicted a war just around the corner; but by this time, France had the backing of Britain and Russia, who made it clear to Bismarck that if war broke out between France and Germany again, it had better be a defensive war on Germany's part, or they would support France.

Bismarck had no particular wish for war of any kind with France, particularly a so-called preventative war, and therefore Germany was careful to give France no fresh reason for resentment. Just in case, however, Bismarck also made a point of excluding France from the careful web of alliances he was creating around Germany, instead encouraging the French to pursue their colonial interests in North Africa. He was particularly concerned that France might ally with Russia, or with Austria, as it had done in the past.

Therefore, despite the fact that Germany still perceived Austria-Hungary as the greatest potential threat to its sovereignty, in order to prevent a French-Austrian alliance, Bismarck pursued an alliance between Germany, Austria-Hungary, and Russia.

This alliance was called the League of the Three Emperors, after emperors Wilhelm I of Germany, Franz-Joseph II of Austria-Hungary, and Alexander II of Russia. It lasted until Germany's relations with Russia began to break down in 1878; Russia was at war with the Ottoman Empire, and Germany did not approve. Bismarck's network of alliances was based on the idea that the constituent nations would not expand their borders or their armies significantly; if Russia began acquiring new territories, everything would be thrown out of balance. But Russia chose to break its alliance with Germany and Austria-Hungary rather than abandon its interests in the east, and as a result Bismarck negotiated the Dual Alliance between Austria-Hungary and Germany, and the Triple Alliance between these two nations and Italy.

Bismarck's Resignation

For the last few decades of the 19th century, Bismarck's diplomatic overtures were highly successful. No further wars broke out on the European continent, and the German empire, in accordance with his plan, was free to grow prosperous, establish foreign colonies, and grow its economy. However, all monarchies have an inherent vulnerability: when power is transferred through a royal line, that is, when kings inherit their thrones rather than being selected based on their qualifications and merits, there is no guarantee that the country will remain in capable hands from one generation to the next. Bismarck had created the Second German Reich, but he did not rule it; he had bequeathed it to Wilhelm I, and thus to the Hohenzollern dynasty. Bismarck believed strongly in the divine right of kings, that is, that the monarch is appointed to rule by God, and he would not have had it otherwise.

When Wilhelm I died in 1888, his son, Frederich III, inherited the throne, but he would only keep it for ninety nine days; he was already suffering from terminal cancer of the throat before his father's death. Frederich III was succeeded by his son Wilhelm II. And Kaiser Wilhelm did not like Bismarck or his policies.

Bismarck was known for the force of his personality; it is noted by scholars that, when he was first made Foreign Minister, he fairly intimidated Wilhelm I into keeping him in office when the Prussian Diet was demanding his removal. Wilhelm II, however, had observed Bismarck's behavior towards his father and grandfather, and was determined to rule his empire without reference to Bismarck's advice.

When drawing alliances between the nations of Europe, Bismarck had taken care to keep Germany on friendly terms with Britain. The Prussian army was unparalleled in Europe, but Germany was a landlocked country, and it had no navy to speak of. Britain, on the other hand, had the most powerful navy in the world. But the Kaiser (both Wilhelm I and Frederich III were *kaisers*, but when "the Kaiser" is mentioned in the historical record, it is always a reference to Wilhelm II) had a peculiar emotional relationship with Britain. His grandmother was Queen Victoria, and he had fond memories of visiting her court and playing with his English relatives as a child.

But Wilhelm II had a difficult, distant relationship with his English mother, and as he grew older his fascination with Britain's naval power developed into something of a rivalry. He wished Germany to develop a powerful navy. More significantly, he was unimpressed by Bismarck's positioning of Germany as a "satisfied" nation—that is, a country that was content to develop its own prosperity and not trouble its neighbors with attempts at invasion and conquest. Wilhelm had a somewhat immature fascination with recreating Prussian military glories of bygone days, and he did not care for Bismarck's careful balance of power or his aversion to wars of expansion.

Bismarck and the Kaiser clashed at increasing volumes over the next two years. Under Wilhelm II's father and grandfather, Bismarck had been permitted to do pretty much as he liked, but the new Kaiser was infuriated by Bismarck's attempts to work around him. Wilhelm II demanded Bismarck's resignation on

March 18, 1890, and Bismarck, outraged but unable to rectify matters, complied.

Bismarck's Legacy

Considering Otto von Bismarck's extraordinary accomplishments and the nearly immeasurable impact he had on the development of Germany and the history of Europe, it is perhaps not surprising that the popular conception of his character was somewhat overblown, more of a legend than an accurate portrait of the man.

Because Bismarck had been the first great proponent of German nationalism, he became, in the decades after his retirement, a kind of mascot for the right wing—that is, the conservative nationalistic parties, of which the Nazis are the most famous example. This is despite the fact that in his career, Bismarck's so called nationalism had served a specific purpose: to rouse a sense of commonality and German identity amongst the German speaking states, so that they would unite to fight the French and remain united as a single German nation thereafter. In other words, to call Bismarck nationalistic was only accurate insofar as it meant that he was primarily concerned with the affairs of his own nation. Once Germany was united and prosperous, Bismarck wished only for it to continue to be so, and was content to manage conflicts with other nations in a peaceful way, through diplomatic negotiations.

The unification of German, however, was a moment in history which naturally loomed large in the myth making of Nazi ideologists; for this reason, its architect could not escape being appropriated by them. It is somewhat ironic that Bismarck was dismissed by the Kaiser for refusing to support his militaristic ambitions, only for the Nazis forty years later to invoke Bismarck's memory in order justify the invasion and occupation of almost all of Europe.

Central to Nazi doctrine—and to Hitler's personal dogma, as laid out in his autobiography—was the notion that greatness for Germany could only be achieved under the rule of a strong single leader whose edicts were not subject to being approved by parliament. Considering that Bismarck's first task for

Wilhelm I was to encourage him to dissolve the Prussian Diet so that he could double the size of the armies without their approval, it is perhaps understandable that the Nazis saw Bismarck as a sort of spiritual forefather of their plans for Germany. But most historians are agreed that Bismarck's belief in the monarch's divine right to rule is inseparable from the actions he undertook to secure absolute power for the king. That is to say, it is not possible to know whether Bismarck would have approved the illegal measures the Nazis used to secure power based simply on the fact that he once violated the Prussian constitution in order to further the king's aims. But it is safe to say that a king, appointed by God, is not the same thing as a Chancellor who declares himself *Führer*.

After Bismarck's dismissal in 1890, the careful balance of powers across continental Europe began to shift. Bismarck's successors as Foreign Minister, to say nothing of the Kaiser himself, did not possess the necessary diplomatic skill to maintain the old alliances and make new ones where necessary. More crucially, the Kaiser and his officer corp were not as eager to avoid war as Bismarck had been, and when a pretext for war presented itself in the form of the assassination of Archduke Franz Ferdinand, the Kaiser's enthusiasm for recreating the glories of past Prussian military victories undoubtedly played a role in pushing matters to a crisis.

Historians today are somewhat conflicted as to whether Bismarck's system of alliances was responsible for the scale of the first World War—it may, for example, have obliged some countries to come to the defense of their allies when they otherwise would have remained neutral. But some scholars believe that Europe was simply ready for a war; too many countries had grown too powerful, and too accustomed to expanding their influence.

Regardless of any contribution Bismarck's work might have made to the development of the First World War, the militarism of the Nazis was a direct inheritance from Kaiser Wilhelm II. That Bismarck was invoked by the Nazis as its figurehead has to do more with their own peculiar way of interpreting history than with reality.

Chapter Two: Germany After the War: Revolution

Now that we have briefly covered the First and Second Reichs, we will be examining, in somewhat greater detail, the decade leading up to Hitler's election as Chancellor of Germany in 1933. Between Bismarck's resignation and the establishment of the German Republic there lies the first World War, but we will not cover it in this book. The events of the war itself are not as crucial to understanding the circumstances which allowed the Nazis to take power as the after effects of the war; but the creation of the German Republic, and the society that developed under its auspices, was inextricably linked with how the Nazi party came to be formed.

The Abdication of Kaiser Wilhelm II

Grandson of Britain's Queen Victoria, last monarch of Germany's 500 year Hohenzollern dynasty, Kaiser Wilhelm II of Germany is remembered by history today in somewhat unflattering terms, particularly with regards to his influence on the events leading to the first World War.

Most accounts of the Kaiser focus on his peculiar and volatile personality. Convinced of his God-given right to rule as supreme autocrat of the German empire, and disdainful of English style democracy, he was given to insisting on his right to make final decisions against the recommendations of his advisors. Though he was considered to be intelligent, he was reported to lack the patience or focus necessary to read complicated reports or documents that would enable him to grasp the nuances of complicated political situations. His impulsive, hot-headed disposition led to a variety of diplomatic disasters, most notably a famous interview with an English newspaper in which he declared that all Englishmen were "mad."

The precise degree to which Kaiser Wilhelm directed Germany's actions in World War I is debatable. Archduke Franz Ferdinand, whose assassination set into motion the chain of events that led to the war, was a close friend of the Kaiser's, and his grief and shock at Ferdinand's death fueled an early determination that Germany would assist in putting down the revolutionary Black Hand group behind the assassination in Bosnia. Once the various treaties and alliances between the European powers began to make apparent the massive scale of the upcoming conflict, Wilhelm made paranoid statements to the effect that he believed that the British were manipulating events on purpose in order to have an opportunity of destroying Germany. Intentionally or not, the Kaiser did his part to aggravate hostilities, and if his attempts to avoid war were sincere, they were nonetheless compromised by his quick temper and his tendency to make decisions of state based on his own volatile emotions.

On the other hand, when it became apparent that the burgeoning conflict could not be de-escalated, and war really was inevitable, the Kaiser was evidently much distressed. As mentioned, he was related closely by blood to George V of England and Nicholas II of Russia, and the idea of fighting both England and Russia appeared to frighten and sadden him. Apparently the Kaiser had been convinced that his familial ties to the various European powers would enable him to peaceably resolve all differences between their countries. Of the conflict between his country and those ruled by his cousins, he was overheard to remark that his grandmother, Queen Victoria, "would not have allowed it!"

When war was irrevocably decided, Kaiser Wilhelm made up for any early misgivings by throwing himself into the role of military warlord with a boyish enthusiasm. "Boyish" is the key word. Though nominally the supreme commander of the German military, the Kaiser lost the support of the Supreme Army Command early in the war, and by the time of Germany's surrender in 1918, the empire was effectively a military dictatorship. Field Marshal Paul von Hindenburg (who would go on to become the President of the German Republic who appointed Hitler as Chancellor) and General Erich Ludendorff directed Germany's military during the war years. They had wanted a war from the beginning, and while they included the Kaiser in military planning during the early period of his enthusiasm, they excluded him more and more from decisions of any importance. The Kaiser excelled in the ceremonial duties of war time, such as giving speeches, reviewing troops, and handing out medals, and his generals made a point of keeping him busy with such tasks.

As the war dragged on, it became increasingly apparent that Germany stood no chance of winning, and more importantly, could no longer support the cost of fighting. National pride was against any idea of a surrender, but Germany was devastated and its people were starving. Consequently, General Ludendorff began discussing the prospect of a negotiated peace with American president Woodrow Wilson.

Wilson's Fourteen Points, a plan for restoring peace to Europe along lines that would not totally devastate an already beleaguered German nation, appealed to Ludendorff. But Wilson, who saw Kaiser Wilhelm as unstable and likely to embroil Germany in more conflicts in the future, made it a condition of Germany's surrender that a democratic government should be instated.

Constitutional changes were made; Germany became a parliamentary democracy. Chancellor Georg van Hertling, a staunch royalist, resigned, and was replaced by the liberal Prince Max von Baden, a member of the royal family who was nonetheless a Social Democrat and far more willing to tolerate the views of the left and make considerations for workers.

This change in the form of government served another useful purpose. Revolution was brewing in Germany. There was a general awareness that the war was all but lost, and the soldiers grew increasingly hostile when they were not demobilized. Many deserted, and many felt deeply betrayed by the military leadership for having wasted their lives and devastated their country to no ultimate end. Consequently, the Supreme Army Command was eager for the democratic government to take power, so that the blame for Germany's surrender could be shifted to its shoulders.

When Wilson was approached with another offer of truce, he laid down three conditions for accepting it.

One of these conditions was that the Kaiser must abdicate, in order to avoid any temptation to reverse the democratic changes that had been made to the government. General Ludendorff's reaction was to attempt to revitalize the war effort; he was removed from power and eventually fled to Sweden. His replacement, Wilhelm Groener, was left to approach Kaiser Wilhelm with the news that his abdication had been demanded, and that Prince Max von Baden had actually already announced it.

Kaiser Wilhelm II of Germany abdicated on November 10th, 1918, and immediately left Germany to live in the Netherlands as a private citizen under the protection of Queen Wilhelmina. He lived in the town of Doorn until his death in June of 1941.

There are conflicting accounts regarding the former Kaiser's feelings about Hitler and the Nazi government. Some evidence indicates that he more or less approved the Nazi doctrine of racial purity and the slaughter and exile of the Jews. Other reports suggest that he was gratified by Nazi assaults against his old enemies, France and England, and sent Hitler the occasional congratulatory telegram.

Before he died, Wilhelm apparently entertained the hope that Hitler would restore the monarchy in Germany; his second wife is known to have written to Hitler encouraging him to do so. But Hitler, crucially, had been a common soldier in the German army during World War I. And as we have mentioned, and will discuss later in more detail, the soldiers who fought in the Kaiser's war felt a good deal of justifiable resentment towards him, and blamed him, in part, for the ruin Germany faced after its surrender.

Nonetheless, Hitler's notion of what was due to Wilhelm II as a symbol of German history led to his burying the Kaiser in a lavish state funeral—adorned, much against Wilhelm's stated wishes in life, by Nazi regalia and Nazi flags.

Armistice

On November 11th, the day after the abdication of Kaiser Wilhelm II, Germany signed an armistice that brought an end to all fighting along the Western front.

The terms of the armistice, which made various demands of Germany, were discussed and debated for the next six months during the course of the Paris Peace Conference. The ultimate result was the Treaty of Versailles.

The terms of the armistice were harsh; much harsher than the Fourteen Point plan proposed by Woodrow Wilson, which had led to the formation of a parliamentary democracy and the abdication of the Kaiser. The principle reason for this lay in the fact that the representatives of the other Allied governments—David Lloyd George in Britain, Georges Clemenceau in France, and Vittorio Orlando in Italy—considered Wilson's terms vague in places and unacceptably lenient in others. The armistice presented to Germany in November of 1918 was punitive, almost absurdly so. Among other things, it demanded that the Germany navy decommission more submarines than it actually owned. But Germany was in no position to demand better terms, and three days after it was placed before German delegation head, Matthias Erzberger, by order of the Supreme Army Command, signed it.

Under the thirty-five provisions of the armistice, Germany was to recall its troops from the various countries where they had been fighting, surrender the vast majority of its munitions, such as cannon, and release all prisoners of war, even though German prisoners of war were not to be released until much later.

The Treaty of Versailles

"The Allied and Associated Governments affirm and Germany accepts the responsibility of Germany and her allies for causing all the loss and damage to which the Allied and Associated Governments and their nationals have been subjected as a consequence of the war imposed upon them by the aggression of Germany and her allies."

Treaty of Versailles, Article 231, Part VIII:
Reparations

The portion of the Treaty of Versailles quoted above (famously known as the "War Guilt" clause) demonstrates pretty clearly the spirit in which it was written, as regards to Germany. It was not sufficient to extract financial compensation for the material losses of the war; Germany must be made to feel how much to blame it had been, rather like a misbehaving child who must be taught to distinguish right from wrong in principle, and not merely by rote. Indeed, the Treaty reads like a long and calculated insult which the governments of the Allied powers knew that Germany had no other option than to accept.

The stated purpose of the earlier armistice was to enable normal relations between the Allied countries and Germany to resume, but while it may have paved the way for official diplomatic relationships to be conducted, nothing like genuine normalcy would be possible under the Allied terms. To call the language used in the Treaty resentful is to put it mildly. Care is taken in the Treaty's wording to point out that Germany "requested" the armistice, and the Allied powers "allowed" it. Since the alternative was

Germany's unconditional surrender and the loss of its autonomy as a nation, the Allied authors of the Treaty must have imagined that the German delegation would swallow any degree of insult and be grateful, and to a certain extent, they imagined correctly.

For a modern reader, it is difficult not to wince when reading the Treaty. And it is all too easy to imagine how the German delegation must have felt. The most powerful nations in the world re-drew the boundaries of the German map, dictated limitations to German interests abroad, restricted its navy and air force, and demanded reparations—even though the first paragraph of Article 232 acknowledges that "the resources of Germany are not adequate, after taking into account permanent diminutions of such resources which will result from other provisions of the present Treaty, to make complete reparation for all such loss and damage." The previous section of the Treaty, entitled "Penalties", even "arraigns" Kaiser Wilhelm II for "a supreme offence against international morality and the sanctity of treaties", and declares the intention of the Allied powers to ask Queen

Wilhelmina of the Netherlands to hand him over for trial. (Despite her refusal to ever meet with the former Kaiser personally, Queen Wilhelmina refused to surrender him, and treated the diplomats who made the request to a stern lecture on the meaning of asylum.)

The outrage which the Treaty produced in Germany was proclaimed from the beer halls to the Reichstag. Germany had not even been permitted to take part in the negotiations, and the declaration that Germany alone bore all the guilt of the war was declared by the German Foreign Minister to be a lie even as he signed it.

The German people referred to the Treaty as the *Diktat,* "dictate", an arbitrary measure which they were forced to accept for fear of the possibility that the Allied nations would otherwise invade. Inquiries into the state of German defenses were made by the government, and only when Field Marshal von Hindenburg declared that Germany had not the slightest hope of defending herself in the event of invasion was it recommended that the Treaty be signed.

German representatives Herman Muller and Joannes Bell signed the Treaty of Versailles on June 28, 1919.

The German Revolution

The ultimate purpose of the measures outlined by the Treaty of Versailles was to cripple German resources to such an extent that there could no longer be any possibility or risk of their instigating another war. Many historians now feel that this was a miscalculation on the part of the Allied powers. When there is a desire to wage war, the means of waging it will be found, and the Treaty of Versailles created just such a desire in the German people. The Treaty was perceived as such an injustice and such a blight upon German honor that by the time the Nazis came to power it was felt that only a second war could restore Germany's credit on the world stage.

Earlier in this chapter we examined the decision made by the Supreme Army Command to allow for the creation of a new liberal government, which served the dual purpose of satisfying America's demands for a permanent democracy in Germany, and providing the German people with a convenient scapegoat on which to pin the blame for the disastrous conclusion of the war. This off-loading of blame from the upper echelons of the military onto the new government and its left wing Chancellor was perhaps more directly responsible for creating the political climate that allowed for the rise of the Nazi party than any other single action by German leaders prior to the founding of the Weimar Republic. By positioning the socialist government as the architect of the armistice, right wing factions such as the Nazi party were able to position themselves as the strong, visionary alternatives to the weaklings who had lost the war for Germany. (The feeling that the new government had betrayed the German people by surrendering was so strong, in fact, that at the end of the second World War, the Allies demanded that the Instrument of German Surrender be signed by no less than the heads of the military, in order to insure that any blame was assigned to the responsible parties.)

The political atmosphere of postwar Germany was intensely strained. In Russia, 1918 was a year of revolution: the tsar, Nicolas II, cousin of Kaiser Wilhelm II, abdicated power and was executed, along with his family, by revolutionary Bolsheviks. Shortly after the Communist government was established in Russia, revolts began breaking out at various levels of German society. The success of the Bolsheviks in Russia lent confident to the Communist uprisings in Germany, but multiple factions representing varying levels of socialist, Communist, and right wing ideologies were also vying for power.

The German Revolution was highly complicated due to the number of political parties and personalities involved. As such, in this book, we will only be examining it in broad outline, so as to provide a context for the establishment of the Weimar Republic, which was the predecessor to the Third Reich and the social landscape in which the Nazi party rose to power.

The "Revolt from Above"

Unlike the Russian revolution, which was heavily ideological and comprehensive in regime change, the German revolution was managed initially by those already in power, namely the Kaiser, who appointed Prince Max von Baden as Chancellor and renounced his own power to appoint ministers, and the Supreme Army Command, who were attempting to establish good will with the Americans so as to secure non-ruinous terms for the armistice that would bring an end to the war.

Von Baden effectively forced the abdication of the Kaiser by announcing it to the Reichstag before the Kaiser had made or announced his decision. Von Baden believed this was a necessary step to avoid a widespread social revolution, which he felt was otherwise inevitable.

Revolt of the Imperial Navy

In the months leading up to the armistice, the soldiers and sailors who had fought for Germany were aware that the war must end shortly. They were anxious for an official declaration of an end to the fighting, and they were unwilling to be dragged into additional fruitless battles when there was no possibility of victory.

In a poorly thought out, last ditch effort to win glory for an all but defeated Germany, the German Imperial Naval Command, under Admiral Franz von Hipper and Admiral Reinhard Scheer, ordered a strike against British forces in ports along the east coast of Scotland. Their orders came without authorization from the new democratic government; it was an order given in the ancient tradition of military men who would rather die fighting than face the dishonor of capitulation.

The result was mutiny and sabotage by the sailors aboard the German war ships involved in the order. The mutiny led to the cancellation of the attack; even though the mutineers were arrested without serious resistance, it had become apparent to the Imperial Naval Command that their forces were not to be relied upon, and only disaster could result from attempting to compel them.

Friedrich Ebert and the Social Democratic Party

Prince Max von Baden's government resigned around the time of the armistice in November of 1918. Von Baden ceded control to the Social Democratic Party under the leadership of Friedrich Ebert. Ebert's government represented a compromise between those who had held power in Germany before the war under the Kaiser, and the new political factions that represented the rights and interests of workers along socialist precepts.

Ebert's government managed to hold power in the face of resistance from revolting communist groups by securing the support of conservative military leaders. In exchange for a promise of social stability, the military threw its weight behind Ebert's government and allowed for highly desired reforms, such as voting rights for every man and woman over the age of twenty, and the eight hour work day.

The Spartacist Revolt

In 1919, Berlin, the capital of Germany, was the site of a series of uprisings, including a general labor strike, known as the January Uprising, or the Spartacist Revolt. It was inspired by the dismissal of the chief of police, Emil Eichorn, who had refused to arrest agitators during a brief rebellion by member of the navy the previous month, known as the Christmas Crisis.

The Spartacus League, named for the leader of a slave rebellion in ancient Rome, was founded by two Marxist intellectuals, Karl Liebknecht and Rosa Luxemburg, who went on to found the Communist Party of Germany in an effort to gain greater support in their efforts to challenge Ebert's government. Longtime critics of the ruling conservative powers in Germany, Liebknecht and Luxemburg had been vocal critics of the war and the Kaiser. It was Luxemburg's wish that Communist party members should influence the government by participating in the new elections, but she was outnumbered by those who felt that the best way to rally the people of Germany to their cause was by inspiring factory workers to create unrest in the streets.

On January 5, 1919, following Eichorn's removal, Liebknecht and others called for a demonstration outside police headquarters. The turnout was much larger than expected; hundreds of thousands of demonstrators staged a temporary occupation of train stations, as well as the offices of right wing newspapers that had called for violent measures to put down Communist agitators. Against the wishes of Luxemburg and the majority of the Communist Party, Liebknecht used the uprising as a platform to call for the overthrow of Ebert's government.

Between January 6th and January 8th, Ebert made a show of attempting to negotiate with Liebknecht and a committee of demonstrators. Liebknecht, however, having called for a general strike on January 7th, was warned the following day that Ebert was making secret arrangements for an unofficial detachment of volunteer soldiers, known as the *Freikorps*, to put an end to the demonstrations by armed assault. Liebknecht called for the Spartacists to defend themselves by taking up arms against the *Freikorps.*

Because the *Freikorps* were mainly soldiers recently returned from the war, they were far better armed than the Spartacists, and they quickly put an end to the revolt. On January 15, 1919, Karl Liebknecht and Rosa Luxemburg were captured by the *Freikorps* and murdered.

Owing to continuing instability in Berlin after the Spartacist Revolt, the government convened in the town of Weimar in February of 1919 to hold a constitutional convention, which lasted until June of 1920. The constitution developed during this period governed Germany until 1933, and technically formed the foundation of government under Nazi rule as well. The Weimar Republic, which governed Germany until Adolf Hitler was elected Chancellor in 1933, derives its name from this.

Chapter Three: Germany Between the Wars: The Weimar Republic

What was the Weimar?

If you aren't especially familiar with German history in the 20th century, it is possible that you have never heard of the Weimar Republic; it was a comparatively brief period of escalating social unrest bracketed by the two World Wars, which vastly overshadow it. But a basic understanding of the changes German society underwent during the Weimar years will provide you with insight into the forces that gave birth to the Nazi party. The Third Reich was in many ways a reaction to the Republic: where Weimar Germany was perceived as soft and decadent, Nazi Germany meant to be strong, ruthless, and scornful of excess.

The Weimar Republic refers to Germany during the years between the end of the Kaiser's rule and the beginning of Hitler's regime, a period which lasted from 1920 to 1933.

If you are not a dedicated history student, you may believe that you have no frame of reference for Weimar Germany; but if you have ever seen the film *Cabaret,* or heard the early music of Marlene Dietrich, or even if you have a vague inkling that at one time Germany was associated with nightclubs, music, literature, and sexual and social permissiveness, then something of the spirit of the Weimar has trickled down through history to reach you, despite the efforts of the Nazi regime to wipe it from memory.

Thanks to the left wing socialist parties that dominated German politics in the early twenties, the Weimar Republic began as a period of intense social change, much of it progressive even by modern standards. The Weimar Constitution, which was adopted in June of 1920, established equal rights for all Germans under the law, regardless of sex or country of origin—which is more than could be said for the official policies of either England, France, or the United States during the same period. Freedom of religion, freedom of speech, the right to privacy, and the right to assembly were all protected by the Constitution in a section entitled, "Basic rights and obligations of Germans," which is similar to the American Bill of Rights.

Despite these social advances, life in Germany during the Weimar period was difficult. The draconian war guilt penalties imposed by the Treaty of Versailles, to say nothing of the resources that Germany had lost, destroyed, or consumed as a result of the war, devastated the economy. The fighting had largely taken place in Belgium and France, rather than in Germany itself, so the means of production—factories and so forth—were not lost, as they would be in the second World War as a result of the bombing. But under the terms of the Treaty, around 30% of formerly German territory, in such places as the Polish corridor and the Alsace-Lorraine, had to be surrendered, which deprived Germany of their resources. And when Germany was unable to pay reparations in a timely manner, France seized more German territory, which exacerbated the problem.

People were unable to find work; many starved. It suited the purposes of the Nazis to lay the majority of the blame for these conditions on the government of the Social Democrats for having surrendered under harsh terms, rather than on the Kaiser and his generals for having pursued an unnecessary war in the first place. (You may remember from the previous chapter that this was precisely what those generals had intended.) Clever Nazi propaganda spread the belief that by accepting the Treaty's punitive terms the government had betrayed the people; the result was a rise in Nazi party membership and an eventual Nazi majority in the Reichstag.

The art, music, films, and dance of the Weimar period are still remembered today, but the image of the Weimar over time has been distorted by the Nazi propaganda surrounding it. Where a discerning modern reader sees positive social change ushered in by socialist principles and a new constitution, the Nazis saw corruption and weakness of mind. For that reason, the Weimar is caricatured more often than it is evaluated, and the Nazi-created image of a perverse, inefficient society lingers today. Such products of the period as the Constitution, however, speak for themselves.

In this chapter, we will examine the Constitution of the Weimar government in some detail, concentrating on its human rights provisions and the limitations it places on the powers of the state. We will also study the weaknesses in its design that were later exploited by Hitler when he was made Chancellor. Afterwards, we will look briefly at economic conditions in Germany during the Weimar, and attempt to make sense of the right wing agenda that motivated the National Socialist party to take power in the early 1930's.

The Weimar Constitution

"The German people, united in its tribes and inspirited with the will to renew and strengthen its Reich in liberty and justice, to serve peace inward and outward and to promote social progress, has adopted this constitution."

Preamble the Reich Constitution of August 11th, 1919

"Instead of working to achieve power by an armed coup, we will have to hold our noses and enter the Reichstag against Catholic and Marxist members. If outvoting them takes longer than outshooting them, at least the result will be guaranteed by their own constitution. Sooner or later we shall have a majority…"

Extract from *Mein Kampf,* by Adolf Hitler, 1923

As we mentioned in the previous chapter, the Constitution of the Weimar Republic was developed during a constitutional convention in the German city of Weimar between February of 1919 and June of 1920. It was signed into law in August of 1920 by the first President of the German republic, Friedrich Ebert, who had previously been appointed Chancellor, replacing Prince Max von Baden. For American readers, the President at this time was the German head of state, equivalent to the Kaiser before him, or the American President, while the position of Chancellor was equivalent to that of the British Prime Minister, who runs the British government under the authority of the head of state, which is the Queen.

During the period of the German Revolution, from 1918 to 1919, Germany had no official head of state—the Chancellor governed Germany by the permission of the former Kaiser's military generals, who enforced their authority through strength of arms, rather than the mandate of the people. The purpose of creating a Constitution was to establish a government that operated by consent of the governed, rather than the mandate of the military.

Germany, like most European nations at the time, had been a monarchy for its entire history. The Weimar Constitution, however, established Germany as a democratic parliamentary republic, with proportional representation by the various political parties. This is somewhat different from the system of government that American readers will be familiar with; German voters in the federal elections voted for the political parties that best represented their interests, and the parties themselves selected the representatives who governed in the Reichstag, or parliament. For instance, if the Social Democratic party received 30% of the vote, then 30% of the parliamentary representatives in the Reichstag would be Social Democrats. This is the system used in countries such as Great Britain in the present day.

There are conflicting views by contemporary scholars as to the viability of the Weimar Constitution; that is to say, whether weaknesses in the Constitution itself doomed the democratic experiment in Germany from its inception, or whether the Weimar Republic's eventual collapse under Nazi rule was simply a testament to the effectiveness of Nazi propaganda and leadership. Certainly the Republic faced opposition and revolt from the beginning, from both left and right wing factions—for example the Communist uprisings in 1919, and the Nazi-led Munich Putsch in 1923. Perhaps most significantly, there was a clause in the Constitution—the now notorious Article 48— which allowed the President of the Republic to bypass democratic process under "emergency conditions"; this provision opened the door to Hitler establishing a Nazi dictatorship after he was made Chancellor in 1933 without technically violating the rule of law.

But in the first federal elections after the war, the overwhelming majority of the votes went to the left wing, democratically minded political parties. And despite the devastating effect of the Treaty of Versailles, the Weimar government overcame problems such as hyperinflation and governed very ably during the early 1920's, in what is sometimes called the "golden age" of the Weimar. For these reasons, a number of scholars believe that after the war, the German people were genuinely invested in establishing a democratic government, and were committed to its success. The view that an eventual overthrow of the Weimar government by nationalistic forces was inevitable (a view taken up in hindsight by some late century observers) seems less an analysis of the social and historical reality of Germany in the 1920's and 1930's, and more a comment upon the enduring power of Nazi propaganda, which viewed their own rise to power as almost pre-destined.

Before we leave the subject of the Weimar Constitution, a brief examination of its articles will help the reader to understand the aspirations the people of Germany had for their country before fascism overtook democracy a few years later. We will also bring some focus to bear on the famous Article 48, which over the years has born so much of the blame for the Nazi takeover of the government.

The Constitution was divided into two main parts, entitled, "Composition of the Reich and its responsibilities", and "Basic rights and obligations of Germans", respectively.

The first part of the Constitution established Germany as a Republic that ruled by the consent of its people, and described the reaches and limitations of the government's power—including respect for the self-determination of other nations (even former German holdings such as Austria), and acceptance of international law as binding on Germany. It also provides for state governments that were distinct from, yet operated under the authority of the federal government, a system similar to that found in the United States today.

The second part of the Constitution declares the equality of men and women before the law, abolishes the privileges of the aristocracy and forbids the creation of more nobles, and also, interestingly, forbids giving out medals. It allowed Germans to leave the country without penalty (a matter of crucial importance to Jews as the Nazis gained influence) and established explicit welfare protections for mothers and their children.

The Constitution of the Weimar Republic was described by journalist Will Shirer as "the most liberal and democratic document of its kind the twentieth century had ever seen." Other historians have taken a less flattering view of it, but the majority of criticism is founded upon one particular provision.

Article 48

Article 48 of the Weimar Constitution reads as follows:

"If a state does not fulfill the obligations laid upon it by the Reich constitution or the Reich laws, the Reich President may use armed force to cause it to oblige.

"In case public safety is seriously threatened or disturbed, the Reich President may take the measures necessary to reestablish law and order, if necessary using armed force. In the pursuit of this aim he may suspend the civil rights described in articles 114, 115, 117, 118, 123, 124 and 154, partially or entirely.

"The Reich President has to inform Reichstag immediately about all measures undertaken which are based on paragraphs 1 and 2 of this article. The measures have to be suspended immediately if Reichstag demands so.

"If danger is imminent, the state government may, for their specific territory, implement steps as described in paragraph 2. These steps have to be suspended if so demanded by the Reich President or the Reichstag. Further details are provided by Reich law."

The original purpose for the inclusion of Article 48 in the Constitution was to enable the President of the Republic to solve urgent problems affecting German society, bypassing legislative proceedings in order to provide relief as quickly as possible. For example, during the hyperinflation crisis, which we will discuss in some detail in an upcoming section of this book, Article 48 was invoked on several occasions in order to implement laws related to taxation, rather than to suspend the civil rights of German citizens

The President's emergency powers under Article 48 were balanced by the Reichstag, which had the power to veto any emergency decree of which it did not approve by a simple majority vote. However, the President, under Article 25 of the Constitution, had the power to dissolve the Reichstag at will and call for new elections. This provision had been created as a tool to bypass parliamentary stalemate and ensure the government continued to function even when rival political parties were unable to work together. But various German presidents used it to clear any opposition posed by the Reichstag to their political agendas. Rather than using it as a tool to work around a Reichstag that could not do its job, the Article began more and more frequently to be used as a tool that enabled the President to avoid working with the parliament.

It was, in fact, one of these Article 25 elections, called by President Paul von Hindenburg at the request of Chancellor Heinrich Bruning in 1930, that paved the way for Hitler's Chancellorship three years later. Bruning asked von Hindenburg to call for a new election in the hopes that it would create a majority vote for a particular bill Bruning was having difficulty passing through the Reichstag. Ironically, the results of the election actually decreased the number of supporters for his bill, and drastically increased the number of Nazi party representatives in the Reichstag.

The Reichstag Fire Decree

Three years later, in 1933, Adolf Hitler was appointed Chancellor of Germany by President von Hindenburg. A mere four weeks after he was sworn in, a Dutch laborer started a fire in the Reichstag building, purportedly to protest the poor treatment of the working class. After several Communist leaders were arrested as co-conspirators, Hitler declared that the fire had been a plot by the Communist party to take over the German government by force. At the time, the Nazis and the Communists were the dominant parties of the Reichstag, meaning that the Communists were positioned to block the nationalistic agenda of the Nazis in parliament. Hitler asked von Hindenburg to declare a state of emergency under the provisions of Article 48 of the Constitution, and von Hindenburg agreed, issuing what became known as the Reichstag Fire Decree on the following day, the 28th of February.

A portion of the text of the Decree is below:

"Articles 114, 115, 117, 118, 123, 124, and 153 of the Constitution of the German Reich are suspended until further notice. Thus, restrictions on personal liberty, on the right of free expression of opinion, including freedom of the press, on the right of assembly and the right of association, and violations of the privacy of postal, telegraphic, and telephonic communications, and warrants for house searches, orders for confiscations as well as restrictions on property are permissible beyond the legal limits otherwise prescribed."

The Decree provided Hitler with such sweeping authority to suspend the civil rights of ordinary citizens at will that it became, in effect, the means by which the Nazis would seize absolute power in Germany. Without the guaranteed protection of free speech, all critics of the Nazi party were liable to arrest. Opposition to the Nazi regime was made illegal before the worst of its crimes were even remotely suspected.

While it is evident that Article 48 of the Weimar Constitution provided Hitler with a tool to aid him in his seizure of power, his use of the Article for that purpose had precedent in the government of the Republic. Had previous Presidents and Chancellors not made a habit of invoking the Article simply to avoid the arduous labor of winning parliamentary support for their agendas, Hitler may or may not have taken that path for himself. Perhaps the road to power was created by Article 48, but it had been smoothed by the footsteps of all the many German leaders who had treaded it before him.

Reparations and Hyperinflation

"My father was a lawyer, and he had taken out an insurance policy in 1903, and every month he had made the payments faithfully. It was a 20-year policy, and when it came due, he cashed it in and bought a single loaf of bread."

Walter Levy

In 1914, prior to World War I, the German mark was backed by the gold standard—this meant that each individual bank note was a symbol for a certain amount of gold held in reserve in the national bank. This came to an end, however, when Germany began borrowing heavily to fund the war. The value of the mark fell. The prices of ordinary items like milk and bread had doubled by 1919.

But the immense task of paying the reparations imposed by the Treaty of Versailles lay before Germany. In 1921, in what has become known as the "London ultimatum", Britain demanded that Germany pay the reparations in a gold backed currency—some other country's currency, in other words. Germany's solution was to print a great number of bank notes in order to buy the foreign money, which it then immediately handed over to other countries. But this caused the value of the mark to drop dramatically.

In 1919, one American dollar was equivalent to about four marks—which put it on about the same level as the currencies of Britain, France, and Italy. By 1921, the value had dropped to 75 marks to one dollar. By January of 1923, one American dollar was worth 7000 marks; eleven months later, at the beginning of November, the dollar was worth over a billion marks. Two weeks later, on November 15th, the mark was one trillion to the dollar; the next day, the 16th of November, it stood at four trillion to the dollar.

Even if you have never read about the hyperinflation at the beginning of the Weimar period before, you may have seen some of the enduring images that came out of the period: children playing with stacks of marks as if they were building blocks, people loading wheelbarrows with piles of bundled bank notes merely to buy a newspaper, people wallpapering their houses with banknotes because the paper it was printed on was more valuable than the currency it represented.

There are astonishing stories of ordinary people trying to go about their daily business when the price of a cup of coffee could double or triple between the moment you ordered it and the moment you went to pay the bill. The mark was so valueless that people of means began to spend as much money as they possibly could, buying anything of value that might replace it: gold, diamonds, jewelry, paintings, pianos, etc. (This practice is known as "flight from currency".) Even so, the market heavily favored the sellers, who likewise began to prefer keeping their items of value to trading them even for unimaginably vast amounts of money.

Workers were paid three times a day because the value of the mark dropped so much between morning and evening that the only way to get any value from money was to spend it the instant you laid hands on it. Wives would wait outside their husbands' workplaces so that the money could be handed over to them immediately, then wait in long lines at the markets to spend the money before the value could drop any further. Very often there was nothing for them to buy, because merchants could not afford to buy merchandise for resale.

The Rentenmark

By the time German currency been devaluated to the point that a trillion marks was equivalent to one American dollar at the end of 1923, cash had become nearly irrelevant to the conduct of daily life. But in spite of the fact that German money was worthless, Germany was a rich country in terms of its assets, which was why it had been possible for the rich to invest their depreciating cash in material items. For the government, there was the land itself, the forests and factories: all of these had value. Such assets could not be liquidated—that is, sold to a foreign country for a hard currency—and liquidity is usually considered a necessary trait of assets that a government uses to back its own currency.

But a stable currency that could replace the *Papiermark* was absolutely necessary. People had lost their life savings, or rather, the amount their savings added up to was now a mere pittance. Anyone living on a fixed income—for instance, a widow living on the proceeds of her husband's life insurance policy—was utterly impoverished. Employer wages at least made some effort to keep up with hyperinflation, but a widow who received 200 marks a month to live did not receive more money when 200 marks stopped being enough money to buy a single slice of bread.

In an effort to curb hyperinflation, a new German bank was established, and a new currency was issued: the *Rentenmark* (named for the new *Rentenbank*.) One *Rentenmark* was worth one billion *Papiermarks*—in effect, the bank had simply knocked the last nine zeroes off the denominations of the new currency. For the first time in years, it became possible to walk into a shop and purchase an item for the price of a single mark.

The *Rentenmark* was a great success—the effect that it had on German society is frequently referred to as "the miracle of the *Rentenmark*"—and yet, the reasons for its success are rather curious.

The first reason for the success of the *Rentenmark*, and the one that is probably easiest for non-economists to understand, is that the German government simply stopped printing money. That is, the banks issued a set amount of money, but they didn't continue to print it whenever they needed more. Printing money to pay their reparation debts was what had got them into trouble in the first place, after all; and the mere fact that it was no longer normal for people to be burdened with so many bank notes that it was cheaper to burn them for heat than to use them to purchase wood went a long way towards restoring the confidence of the German people.

The confidence of the German people is, in effect, the second reason that the *Rentenmark* succeeded, and this is the factor that baffles to this day.

Apart from the fact that prices deflated to reflect the adjusted value of the *Rentenmark* in comparison to the *Papiermark*, the *Rentenmark* was publicized as a currency that had proper government backing—not gold backing, but backing in hard assets, at least. This was not, precisely, an untruth, but as previously mentioned, these assets were non-liquid: land, buildings, things that could not be sold or traded. Nonetheless, the mere idea that this currency, unlike the last one, stood for something real, was enough to make it successful. The German people treated it as if it value, and therefore it functioned as if it had value.

The *Rentenmark* was a temporary currency. In 1924 it was replaced by *Reichsmarks*, which remained the official currency of Germany until after the end of World War II. One *Reichsmark* was equal to one *Rentenmark*, but the *Reichsmark* had a gold standard backing of 30%, which made it competitive in the international marketplace. Tax rates increased, and from 1924 to 1925 the German government had surplus revenue. But the lives of ordinary citizens had been irrevocably altered. Those who lost their life savings were never compensated, and for the entire country, the illusion that life in Germany could return to normal after the war was shattered.

The Dawes Plan and the Young Plan

Due to the hyperinflation crisis, which had been triggered by the London ultimatum (Britain's demand that all reparations must be paid in gold standard currency) Germany had begun to default on its reparation payments by 1923; she could not provide the coal, timber, or other resources to cover the deficiency of cash payments. As retribution for the failure to pay, French and Belgian troops seized control of and occupied the Ruhr valley, one of Germany's chief industrial centers. To protest the occupation by foreign troops, German workers in the Ruhr region went on strike, which brought industrial production to a standstill. The strike had the support of Germans outside the region, but it further reduced her ability to make reparation payments.

In an effort to forestall what was now a building international crisis, American bankers, under the leadership of American banker Charles G. Dawes, formulated the Dawes Plan to ease Germany's reparations burden. As of August 1924, bankers from the United States, under the guidance of the State Department, loaned Germany 800 million marks, and in return Germany was required to begin reparation payments of one billion marks per year for five years, after which the rate was raised to two and a half billion marks per year. The French and Belgian troops occupying the Ruhr valley region agreed to evacuate and cede the territory back to German control, and the national bank of Germany was re-organized with advice and assistance from American economists. The Dawes plan was highly regarded by the international community, and Charles Dawes won the Nobel prize on the strength of it. Dawes would later go on to become Vice President of the United States under Calvin Coolidge.

By 1929, when the amount of Germany's reparation payments was set to more than double, it was recognized that the terms of the Dawes Plan were insupportable, even with the German economy in a state of recovering prosperity. As a result, Rockefeller Foundation trustee Owen D. Young devised a new plan. The Young Plan reduced Germany's annual reparations payments to one third of the original set amount. Over the next 59 years, Germany would be responsible for making payments totaling 112 billion gold standard marks (an amount equivalent to 8 billion U.S. dollars), with the understanding that should Germany ever find itself in a position where it was capable of paying the entire original amount without devastating its own economy, it would do so.

Had Germany abided by the terms of the Young Plan as they were originally set out, the period of its reparations payments would not have ended until 1988. But the stock market crash of 1929 put an end to it. The generous loans which had been offered to Germany by American bankers who had hoped Germany would develop into a prosperous trading partner had to be recalled, and as a consequence, the Allied nations agreed not to hold Germany responsible for further reparations until the global economy had recovered. At the same time, right wing political groups in Germany, most notably the National Socialist party, had formed such an opposition to the Treaty of Versailles that in 1929 they proposed a law that would criminalize the payment of reparations. The so-called "Liberty Law" was put to a referendum vote, which passed, but was voted down in the Reichstag.

The psychological trauma which the burdens of reparations and the chaos of hyperinflation inflicted on the German people during this period of the Weimar era is held by many scholars to have played a significant role in creating the societal conditions which enabled the Nazi party to come to power in 1933. Hyperinflation in particular dealt a severe blow to the German ethos of hard work and frugality. After the first World War, there had been a belief, or a hope, that if ordinary people kept their heads down and continued to do their jobs and live their lives in the traditional way, normalcy would be restored, and the country would be all right. But the absurd realities created by hyperinflation—such as burning money for fuel—seemed to contradict this hope. The German people felt powerless, their lives devastated by economic forces that no amount of hard work could withstand, and which even educated people could make no sense of, let alone factory workers and housewives.

The German writer, Thomas Mann, wrote of this period:

"The market woman who without batting an eyelash demanded 100 million for an egg lost the capacity for surprise. And nothing that has happened since has been insane or cruel enough to surprise her."

By "nothing that has happened since", Mann was of course referring to the escalating horrors that began to be perpetrated by the Nazis immediately upon their gaining power. The economic chaos of the Weimar period had, in a very real way, taken the fight out of the German people. It is therefore perhaps not so terribly surprising that in the first election following the peak of the hyperinflation crisis in 1923, the National Socialist party gained 32 seats in the Reichstag. After all, the Nazis were promising things that the Social Democratic government could not: an end to reparations, and even more temptingly, compensation to all those who had lost their savings and income to hyperinflation.

The Golden Age of the Weimar

In the next chapter, we leave the Weimar period behind and shift our focus to the early years of the Nazi regime. But just in case the picture we have painted of financial collapse, poverty, and social chaos in the Germany of the 1920's has created the impression that there was little of good that was lost when the Nazis took power, we should focus at least briefly on the positive effects that a democratic government and a liberal constitution had on society after the first World War.

In 1923, Gustav Streseman became Chancellor of Germany. It was under his leadership that the

Rentenmark was introduced and hyperinflation was curbed. He was not universally popular; his acceptance of the Dawes Plan meant that many, especially on the far right, perceived him as a supporter of the Treaty of Versailles and a lackey of the French. However, due to his willingness to cooperate with other global powers, he was awarded the Nobel peace prize, and Germany was admitted as one of the chief members of the League of Nations, which gave them an influence in deciding world affairs that the British and the French, for example, were not especially pleased by. Streseman's Chancellorship only last for 100 days, but he served as Germany's foreign minister from 1924-1929, the period which is now considered the golden age of the Weimar. His work in re-establishing Germany as a member of a global community, a country with which other nations were willing to deal on terms of equality, was his enduring legacy and was responsible for creating relative stability in Germany during the Weimar era.

During Streseman's Chancellorship and afterwards, the democratic and socialist aims of the Weimar Constitution were put into action via a series of sweeping social reforms which greatly improved the quality of life for the German people. Labor reforms in the shape of an 8 hour workday and a 36 hour weekend were implemented. People who could not work to support themselves, such as widows and their children, and the disabled, including war veterans and their dependents, received government assistance and health insurance. Taxes for the wealthy increased, which lightened the burdens of the poor. Child welfare laws were enacted, including laws which gave all children the right to a free education.

In addition to social reforms, the culture which developed during the Weimar era is still famous today for its paintings, literature, music, films, and its striking aesthetic. Intellectuals, philosophers, scholars, artists, and scientists from around the world flocked to Berlin, which had developed into the international center of innovation and culture. Public universities in Germany flourished during this period.

In 1918, Jews were given full admittance to the universities for the first time, and as a result, Berlin became a gathering place for Jewish intellectuals. It was an important period in the development of Marxist theory, supported by the powerful Communist political parties who gained significant numbers in the Reichstag between the wars.

Germany during the Weimar was the birthplace of the German Expressionist movement, which created an abundance of art, literature, film, and music. Movies produced in Germany during this period include early experiments in psychological horror, such as *The Cabinet of Doctor Caligari,* and *Nosferatu,* as well as science fiction movies such as *Metropolis*, and the romantic film *The Phantom of the Opera,* all of which are still studied today as some of the most important achievements of the silent film era. Expressionist painters such as Otto Dix employed stark colors, brutal tones, and eerie, abstract imagery to represent the psychological disconnect experienced by soldier returning home after the war. Writers such as Thomas Mann and Erich Maria Remarque were active during this period, and British novelist Christopher Isherwood penned Cabaret, perhaps the most famous and enduring picture of life in the Weimar known today. Composer Arnold Schoenberg, innovator of atonal styles in music and inventor of the twelve-tone technique, produced frightening, yet beautiful operas that reflected the uncertainty and confusion of life in Germany after the war.

Today, Weimar Berlin is invoked as a byword for "decadence", a reputation which was created as much by the economic situation after the war as by the remarkable flourishing of the arts. In every country which saw the return of soldiers from the war, notions surrounding propriety, the role of women, sexual orthodoxy, religion, and marriage were beginning to relax from their rigid 19th century constraints. In Germany in particular, hyperinflation had done damage to the traditional expectations young people had been raised with. After all, there was no point in getting a job when money was worthless, and it was impossible to settle down and raise a family without money. For all of these reasons, young people felt that it was impossible to follow the example of their parents. The world was falling down around their ears—better to spend such money as they had in enjoying themselves.

Berlin became famous for its "underground" culture of nightclubs, prostitution, and sexual experimentation. With so many young women, and young men, lacking any other means of supporting themselves, sex work became almost normal in certain parts of the city. The German government, in an effort to check the spread of syphilis, which had reached epidemic proportions during the war, had established state sponsored brothels for soldiers, which operated under the supervision of doctors. German soldiers were given special rations which could be exchanged for sexual services at these brothels, and as a result, many soldiers returned home having grown accustomed to visiting sex workers as a matter of course. At the height of the Weimar period, there were approximately five hundred venues for sexual entertainment in Berlin, including establishments that catered exclusively to gay men, lesbians, and alternative sexual identities. Cocaine use was also widespread during this period.

Examination of these aspects of Weimar society and culture provides an illuminating perspective on the rhetoric employed by Hitler and the Nazis. Their propaganda painted them as the saviors of a weak, corrupted Germany that had lost its morals and its spine, preferring to indulge in drugs and sexual licentiousness rather than stand up to the bullying influence of other countries that were extorting reparation payments and sapping Germany of its former greatness.

In the eyes of Hitler, the Germany of the past had been the Germany of world-dominating empires, respected and feared by the very nations that now wielded the Treaty of Versailles like a cudgel to beat Germany into submission. He felt that the German race, which had created the Holy Roman Empire under Charlemagne, had come under pestilential influences—the Communists who opposed the Nazis in the Reichstag, chief among them. To the Nazis, Communism carried an essential taint of

Jewishness—Marx was a Jew, and the growing ranks of Jewish intellectuals in the German universities were often Marxist.

Demonstrating a lack of any nuanced understanding of their own recent history, the Nazis conflated every ill affecting German society—the disastrous and dishonorable ending of the war, the moral insult of the War Guilt clause in the Treaty of Versailles, the sapping of the economy under reparation payments, and the misery of Germans who had lost their savings due to hyperinflation. All problems affecting Germany were, to the Nazis, one problem—which might be phrased as the loss of German pride—and it had one cause: the liberals and Jews and Communists who had betrayed Germany at the end of the war, and who had gone on to corrupt the nation with their weak-minded ideals, producing a generation which could not restore Germany to greatness, until they had been "purified" by the Nazi agenda.

In the following chapter, we will begin to examine the methods by which the Nazis established dominance over Germany, beginning with the rise of the National Socialists, the Munich Putsch, and culminating in the appointment of Hitler as Chancellor of Germany in 1933.

Chapter Four: The Dawn of the Nazi Party

Early Years of Adolf Hitler's Political Career

Adolf Hitler was a decorated veteran of the first World War, holding the rank of private. He had volunteered to serve in the German army, despite having been born in Austria in 1889. (As a reminder of the historical context, this was the year before Otto von Bismarck resigned as Kaiser Wilhelm's Foreign Minister.) Hitler's family had moved to Bavaria when he was a child, and Hitler renounced his Austrian citizenship in 1925; he served in the German army as a foreign volunteer.

Hitler's political career began after the end of World War I. Lacking other job prospects, he stayed in the army and was assigned as an intelligence officer tasked with infiltrating the German Workers' Party, to monitor it for subversive anti government activity. However, Hitler was attracted to the policies that the Worker's Party espoused, and after he had attended a number of meetings and given a few rousing speeches, the party leader invited him to become a member.

During his first years in the German Worker's Party, Hitler would meet Dietrich Eckart, who would become his mentor; the book Hitler wrote in prison a few years later, *Mein Kampf*, would be dedicated to Eckart.

Munich Putsch

In 1920, the German Worker's Party changed its name to the National Socialist German Worker's party; the word "Nazi" comes from an abbreviation of the first two words in the German version of the name, *Nationalsozialistische*.

Earlier in this book we examined the various revolts that troubled Germany in the early years of the Weimar Republic. Many of the earlier revolts, such as the Spartacist Uprising, came from left wing political parties like the Communists; but these uprisings quieted after the Weimar Constitution was adopted, due to the fact that the left wing parties began to see large numbers of their own representatives elected to the Reichstag.

The liberal Weimar government treated compliance with the Treaty of Versailles as a necessary evil, one which Germany could not avoid for risk of a potential invasion by Britain or France, which Germany could not defend itself from. But as the economic fallout of the reparations payments triggered the hyperinflation crisis, right wing uprisings began to crop up throughout the country in their turn.

It is important to remember that Germany was still a fairly new country. Many people in 1918 had been alive during the Franco-Prussian War; they were among the people whom Bismarck manipulated into uniting behind Prussia and going to war against France, by using the press to stir up a huge tide of nationalistic, anti French sentiment. A mere generation ago, Germany had been the conqueror of France. The Second German Empire had been officially declared in the palace of Versailles itself, and the Treaty of Versailles of 1871 had united the German nation, seized Alsace-Lorraine from France, and imposed reparations on France that had to be paid before Prussian troops agreed to withdraw from the country.

Seen in this light, it is perhaps not surprising that some Germans were scarcely able to abide the reversal of fortunes they suffered after their defeat in the first World War, a mere forty seven years later. France was now the conqueror. The second Treaty of Versailles, which was designed to humble Germany so completely that it could never again make war in Europe, bore the same name as the Treaty which had created the second German Reich. The humiliation was severe, multi-layered, and not to be borne, as far as conservative thinkers in Germany were concerned. Repudiating the Treaty of Versailles was the principle platform on which right wing political parties in Germany ran during the early 1920's, and it was with that goal in mind that the Nazi party staged an attempted putsch, or coup, in Bavaria in 1923.

Bavaria was one of the four kingdoms which had united to create the German nation-state in 1871, and Munich was its capital; it was in Bavaria that Hitler eventually obtained his German citizenship. On November 8, 1923, Hitler, accompanied by Nazi party members, interrupted a speech being given by the state commissioner of Bavaria in a Munch beer hall. He announced that a new nationalist revolution was underway, and would soon spread across the country from Munich to Berlin.

By this point, the Nazis, like other political organizations in Germany during the mid twenties, had established its own private security force: the SA, Stormtroopers, or Brownshirts, as they would become known. (All Nazi party members wore uniforms at meetings and rallies, as a way of emphasizing the Prussian military legacy they saw themselves as upholding, but the Stormtroopers were actually armed and organized as a paramilitary force.) Hitler, with the

SA at his back, attempted to seize various government centers in Munich over the course of the next day, such as police stations and post offices. But Hitler had been counting on the cooperation of the Bavarian state commissioner, and therefore the official police, in order to hold onto the parts of the city they had seized and spread the revolution onwards. He did not receive this support; the state commissioner defected as soon as Hitler was no longer holding him at gunpoint.

November 9th was a date with tremendous symbolic value for the German people; a number of events significant in history had taken place on that day. For Hitler, the choice of date was a reference to the day when Prince Max von Baden had declared the abdication of the Kaiser and the formation of the democratic socialist government in 1918. Hitler and other right wing nationalists considered this act to have marked the beginning of Germany's ruin and disgrace. Those responsible for the formation of the republic were referred to by the Nazis as the

"November criminals". Therefore it was on November 8th that Hitler announced the nationalist revolution; the plan was that the Nazis would have taken over all of Munich on the 9th. Instead, the attempted coup failed categorically, and November 9th became the date Hitler was arrested.

Hitler was tried and sentenced to five years in prison for high treason. But even in 1923, such was Hitler's popularity that he served less than one year of his sentence. During the period of his incarceration he was treated favorably by his guards, who permitted him to receive visitors and dictate his autobiography, *Mein Kampf*, to an assistant, Rudolph Hess. By the time he was released, Hitler had resolved that in the future, the Nazi party would achieve power through democratic means, via public elections.

The Referendum of 1929

When Hitler was released in 1925, conditions in German society had ceased to be favorable to the growth of the Nazi party. In 1923, the year of the putsch, the country had been at the peak of the hyperinflation crisis; chaos was the order of the day. But by the time Hitler left prison, the golden age of the Weimar had arrived; the *Rentenmark* and the Dawes Plan had restored order, and the German economy was recovering. The liberal government was popular and effective, and right wing nationalist groups were left to bide their time and wait until the political climate was ripe again.

Because conditions had improved so much, the Nazi party did not hold much appeal for the middle class, and it struggled to get coverage for its views in mainstream newspapers. In the mid 1920s, the Nazis were still considered too extreme to be taken seriously, even by other right wing parties like the German National People's Party. Nonetheless, Hitler's reputation as a stirring orator was gaining him a certain amount of respect and notice. His ability to energize a crowd was so feared by government officials that he had been temporarily banned from speaking in public in Bavaria after the Munich putsch.

The Wall Street stock market crash of October 29, 1929, created the opportunity the Nazi party had been waiting for. Germany had barely recovered from the hyperinflation crisis when the failure of the banks forced thousands of businesses to close, destroying millions of German jobs in the process. The level of panic was unprecedented, and the Nazis were quick to capitalize on the desire of all panicking people to turn to firm leadership.

In the last chapter we discussed the Dawes Plan and its successor, the Young Plan: they were organized efforts by American bankers and financiers to alter the terms on which Germany paid reparations, in a way that did not place so much strain on its economy. The Young Plan was considered to be favorable to Germany—far more favorable than the British or French were entirely pleased with—and as such, it was popular amongst the German people. But right wing nationalists were opposed to the payment of any reparations on principle, and the stock market crash of 1929 forced this debate to a crisis.

Alfred Hugenberg, prominent nationalist politician and head of a media empire, was the architect of a law which he wished to bring before the Reichstag for a vote. This law would not only end the payment of reparations and repudiate the Treaty of Versailles, it would make it punishable by law for any German official to cooperate with demands for reparations. It was known as the Liberty Law, or the Law Against the Enslavement of the German People.

Hugenberg had formed a committee of political elites to support the Liberty Law, but for it to have any hope of succeeding in the Reichstag, it would need to gain popular support. This would require speeches and campaigns, grassroots political endeavors that Hugenberg and his colleagues were not at all accustomed to conducting. For this reason, Hugenberg invited Hitler to cooperate with his cadre of conservative politicians, the Reich Committee for the German People's Petition.

This invitation was issued somewhat to the dismay of Hugenberg's colleagues. In 1929, the Nazi party did not participate in national politics at the same level as the other conservatives parties—and if their views received any coverage in a newspaper, it was only as the punchline to a political cartoon. But the Nazis were perceived as having a particular appeal to young Germans, and no one else in German politics had Hitler's talent for persuading an audience through speechmaking.

For Hitler, cooperation with Hugenberg gave the Nazi party access to a great deal of money, sympathetic coverage in the one hundred and fifty newspapers Hugenberg owned, and most importantly, legitimacy. During the campaigns to gather votes, the Nazis were treated as a serious political party with valuable contributions to make in government. The Law Against the Enslavement of the German People failed; only 14% of Germans showed up to vote for it, well below the 51% required to bring a referendum before the Reichstag. (Over 90% of those who voted in the referendum were in favor of the law, however, which shows that they were probably mostly driven to the polls by Hitler's campaigns.) The Young Plan was officially ratified by the Reichstag in 1930, although the stock market crash would result in the recall of the huge American cash loans which would have made the plan possible.

Despite the defeat of the Liberty Law countermeasure, the Nazis benefited greatly from their partnership with Hugenberg and their association with the more mainstream conservative factions in German politics. As a result of his campaigns and the press coverage he received, by the end of 1929, Hitler was famous.

Roots of Nazi Anti-Semitism

Before we advance any further in the timeline of the Nazi takeover of Germany, let us pause to clarify some of their motivations and intentions pertaining to matters other than their opposition to the Treaty of Versailles.

In the present day, Nazism is a byword for anti-semitism, or the hatred of Jewish people. Most people alive today were born after the Holocaust and the founding of the modern state of Israel, and as a result there is a certain lack of understanding as to the historical position of Jews in Europe. Contemporary students of history are sometimes under the impression that the persecution of Jews was a practice unique to, or originating with the Nazis, but this is far from the case. Anti-Jewish bigotry had been practiced in Europe for centuries. In certain regions, at certain times, Jews were given comparatively equal status with Christians, but elsewhere they were forbidden from holding public office, confined to specific areas of the cities in which they lived, and subject to sudden, legally sanctioned outpourings of violence.

There are a number of reasons for this, or rather, pretexts, one of which has particular relevance to the

Nazi paranoia about the Jewish people. In Europe, during the Middle Ages and the Renaissance, Christians were forbidden by the Church to collect interest on loans, a practice which was termed usury and forbidden by scripture. As a result, Jews played an important role in business; they could act as moneylenders, a practice which is only profitable when interest can be collected, and without which merchants could not conduct their business.

But this created resentment amongst Christians, who perceived the Jews to whom they owed money as growing rich at their expense. Jews were despised anyway, as any minority race or religion is despised by those who see them as different, and their work as moneylenders served as a convenient excuse to despise them more. In the modern age, a few Jewish families in Europe became prominent in the banking industry; they were, of course, vastly outnumbered by Christian bankers, who since the Reformation were no longer constrained by usury laws, but the paranoid notion that a conspiracy of Jews controlled all the banks in Europe was popular in Germany in the early part of the century. Indeed, so ancient and deeply rooted is this myth that it is still possible to find people who are misguided enough to believe it.

As a result of this, the Nazis found fertile ground for their propaganda asserting that mysterious Jewish bankers operating in secret somehow controlled the national purse strings. You may also remember from our examination of the social reforms made in Germany during the Weimar period that, after the first World War, certain restrictions that had been placed on German Jews during the 19th century were lifted. Because they were now permitted to attend the universities, Jewish intellectuals (like intellectuals around the world) flocked to Berlin to participate in the city's flourishing artistic, political, literary, and philosophical culture. Such liberties infuriated many German conservatives, not at all dissimilarly to how the sight of a Muslim person in hijab infuriates some conservatives in the United States and other western countries today.

The Dolchstoßlegende

Latent, long-standing anti Jewish bigotry in Germany, compounded with conservative denial regarding the true reasons for Germany's defeat at the end of the first World War, produced a belief which is known today as the "stabbed in the back" legend, or the *Dolchstoßlegende*. It was already extant prior to the formation of the Nazi party, but it formed the basis for a great deal of Nazi ideology and propaganda; Hitler wrote about it extensively in *Mein Kampf*.

The principle cause of Germany's defeat in World War I is generally held to be the entry of the United States into the war. The fresh infusion of healthy troops pushed the German lines back in a one hundred day offensive, at the end of which the Germany army was out of virtually all resources needed to conduct a war. But this did not constitute an adequate explanation for defeat to many Germans. They saw the abdication of the Kaiser, the declaration of the republic, the signing of the armistice, and the acceptance of the Treaty of Versailles as one long campaign of treachery against the German people, organized by a conspiracy of Bolsheviks (fresh from overthrowing the government of Tsar Nicholas II of Russia), weak-willed politicians, and Jews, who were supposedly not only controlling the banks, but had infiltrated the German army as looters and spies.

The theory itself, as well as the phrase "stabbed in the back", originated with General Erich von Ludendorff, one of the heads of the Supreme Army Command, and was quickly taken up by his colleagues, such as Paul von Hindenburg, out of a desire to find a scapegoat for their own failures. A popular book published in 1919, entitled *The Jew in the Army*, further propagated this belief. This myth was repeated in newspapers and in public discourse, and it was impossible to disprove; the facts pertaining to the state of the German army, and the poor decisions made by Germany's military dictatorship during the war, were simply unconvincing to those who were invested in the belief that Germany had been poised for victory in 1918.

The fact that some prominent Jewish political writers had written articles opposing the war was seen as proof of the intent of Jews to sabotage Germany's chances. Jews, generally, were considered to be among the so called "November criminals" who had formed the German republic and accepted the terms of the Treaty of Versailles. Because the status of Jews had been elevated during the Weimar Republic, they were perceived to be among those who had benefited from Germany's defeat. In reality, more than twelve thousand Jews serving in the Germany army had died in defense of their country during the first World War. But Hitler had learned early in his political career that weary, defeated German soldiers, who wanted to understand why they had suffered and fought for no result, would lend eager ears to his scapegoating of Jews, and it became a favored propaganda theme during his rise to power.

After Hitler became Chancellor of Germany in 1933,

the Nazi regime stripped German Jews of most of their civil rights and instituted a boycott of Jewish owned business. The Nazis instituted a campaign of gradually escalating intimidation and financial persecution against the Jewish population, culminating in the "Final Solution", a plan of systematic genocide against European Jews from approximately 1941 to 1945.

Hitler Becomes Chancellor of Germany

Between 1929 and 1933, the Nazi party began to make significant gains in German national elections, resulting in their gaining partial control of the Reichstag. While they did not have a clear majority during any period prior to 1933, neither did any of the other parties. Their chief opponents in parliament were the Communist party, which led to a parliamentary stalemate; being diametrically opposed in their ideologies and aims, there was no possibility of their forming a coalition and working effectively together. The centrist parties in the Reichstag considered a Nazi government preferable to a

Communist takeover, so they threw their support behind Hitler. However, when the Nazi party gained 37% of the seats in the Reichstag in the election of 1932, President Paul von Hindenburg (former member of the German Supreme Army Command in World War I) was unwilling to name Hitler as Chancellor, despite the fact that this position was normally given to the leader of the dominant party.

Hindenburg named two different men as Chancellor in 1932: Franz von Papen, then Kurt von Schleicher. But neither Chancellor was capable of ending the parliamentary stalemate. As a result, Papen, wishing to regain some measure of power, gathered a group of influential Germans, including Alfred Hugenberg and Nazi industrialists, who made a formal request of Hindenburg that he instate Hitler as Chancellor, with Papen to serve under him as Vice Chancellor. Hindenburg acceded to the request, and Hitler was named Chancellor on January 30, 1933.

For a brief period of time, Hitler worked within the

democratic process, forming a coalition with the nationalistic German National People's Party. But in February of 1933, the Reichstag Fire, and the resulting Reichstag Fire Decree, which we discussed in an earlier chapter, led to the dissolution of the Reichstag and Hitler's acquisition of emergency powers. The immediate effect was the suppression of the Communist party in Germany. The long term effect was the creation of the Third Reich and Hitler's naming himself the Führer, or dictator of Germany.

Chapter Five: The Third Reich Begins

The Enabling Act of March 1933

"In the course of the past fourteen years, our Volk has suffered deterioration in all sectors of life, which could inconceivably have been greater. The question as to what, if anything, could have been worse than in these times is a question which cannot be answered in light of the basic values of our German Volk as well as the political and economic inheritance which once existed.

In spite of its lack of mobility in political feelings and positions, the German Volk itself has increasingly turned away from concepts, parties, and associations which, in its eyes, are responsible for these conditions.

The number of Germans who inwardly supported the Weimar Constitution in spite of the suggestive significance and ruthless exploitation of the executive power dwindled, in the end, to a mere fraction of the entire nation."

Extract from Hitler's speech before the Reichstag,
March 23, 1933

The Reichstag Fire Decree suspended civil liberties in
Germany and authorized Hitler to forbid government
criticism in the press, persecute Communist party
members, and block legally elected Communist
Reichstag representatives from participating in
government. Thus, having excluded his most
dedicated and numerous political opponents from the
democratic process, Hitler gave a speech before
parliament proposing a constitutional amendment
entitled the Enabling Act, or the Law to Remedy the
Distress of People and Reich. It would, in effect,
extend the President's Article 48 emergency powers
by giving the Cabinet (and thus the Chancellor)
power to act without Reichstag approval for a period
of four years, after which the Act would have to be re-
approved.

Not content with having banned Communist party
representatives from the vote, Hitler filled the voting

chamber with members of the SA, the Nazi party's private militia, in an intimidating display of martial power. He also used the provisions of the Reichstag Fire Decree to prevent as many representatives as possible of the other left wing opposition parties, such as the Social Democrats, from entering the chamber, for so called security reasons. Some opposition party members chose to flee Germany at this point, sensing the inevitability of deadly persecution once Hitler gained unrestricted powers. In the end, the Social Democrats were the only party which opposed passage of the Enabling Act, which was confirmed with 83% of the vote.

Hitler's Opponents Silenced

While the role that Nazi concentration camps played in the Holocaust is notorious, there is a popular misconception that they were built only after the Final Solution began to be implemented. In fact, the very first concentration camp, Dachau, was built in 1933 to house political prisoners—and, even more chillingly, to train SS officers how to dehumanize prisoners so that they could inflict violence on their captives without hesitation or remorse. After Dachau was expanded to include forced labor subcamps, it became the model on which all future concentration camps were based. Among those imprisoned in Dachau during the early years of the Nazi regime were Jews, Communists, homosexuals, and Jehovah's Witnesses, as well as "social misfits": the homeless and chronically unemployed, drug users and alcoholics, sex workers, Rom people ("gypsies"), and Catholics who resisted the Nazi infiltration of the churches.

Other draconian measures to silence critics of the Nazis were undertaken in 1933. Under the provisions of the Reichstag Fire Decree, Hitler instituted Special Courts to try political dissidents, claiming that the civilian justice system was not equipped to deal with them. The Special Courts were authorized under the Decree to Protect the Government of the National Socialist Revolution and the Law for the Guarantee of Peace Based on Law.

Gleichschaltung

In our examination of the Weimar period, we briefly covered culture in Berlin in the late twenties, which had been affected by a combination of relaxing social attitudes towards sexuality and the role of women, as well as by severe economic conditions which altered traditional values. We also made reference to the Nazi belief that liberal Weimar society was decadent and corrupted and required "purification". The process by which the Nazis attempted this purification involved banning Jews from most arenas of public life, expelling women from universities and professions, and staging symbolic public book burnings to create public unity against "un-German" influences in arts and culture. The desired product of these actions was called *Gleichschaltung*, meaning a unity or uniformity of ideology across all aspects of life. In a practical sense, *Gleichschaltung* meant that it wasn't sufficient for Germans to demonstrate perfect compliance with Nazi edicts; they were required to adopt Nazi ideology and display the fervor of true believers.

One such symbolic book burning took place in May of 1933. Around 40,000 people, many of them university students, burned over 25,000 books under the supervision of Hitler's propaganda minister, Joseph Goebbels. Foreign books, books by Jewish authors, and books propagating ideas such as racial equality, parity of the sexes, or rights for the disabled, were destroyed along with any books deemed pornographic in nature.

The demand for ideological uniformity also meant that, shortly after the Nazi takeover, only Nazi party members were permitted to join organizations or hold positions of power or responsibility, including receiving work promotions. German youth organizations were founded to inculcate Nazi beliefs in children and teenagers: the *Deutches Jungvolk* and Hitler Youth for boys, and the *Jungmädel* and League of German Young Women for girls. Even for adults, most recreational activities, such as football or chess, were conducted through official Nazi sponsored clubs.

By emphasizing community activities in this way, German citizens could be carefully watched, as well as encouraged to monitor one another. Perhaps more importantly, the deliberate stripping away of all personal freedoms could be disguised as something other than what it was—something positive and uplifting, rather than a dangerous attempt to separate German citizens from the protection of the law against state interference.

Racial Hygiene and Early Persecution of Jews
The first planned, coordinated act of persecution against the Jews in Germany came about as a means of punishing Jews for resisting the incremental, escalating persecution they had been subjected to up to that point. German newspapers would not print stories that were sympathetic to Jewish suffering, or even stories that reported it objectively—in fact, the newspapers were frequently the source of editorials which called for attacks on Jews in the first place.

Jews and non Jews alike outside of Germany were concerned by the rumors that were circulating about how an entire segment of Germany's population was being mistreated; they printed articles and interviewed German Jews in an attempt to draw the world's attention to their predicament. Within Germany, Jews had also carried out small scale boycotts of businesses owned by Nazi party members.

Curiously, despite the fact that the Nazis persecuted Jews throughout their regime, they had no wish to be *seen* to be doing so. Even during the design of the Final Solution, overt reference was never made to the slaughter of Jews; murderous intent was communicated primarily by euphemism. Hitler was particularly anxious for Germany's image in the foreign press at the beginning of his regime. Therefore, in April of 1933, a wide scale, state sponsored, Nazi boycott of Jewish businesses was implemented in retaliation. Armed and uniformed SA troops stationed themselves in front of Jewish owned department stores and shops, as well as professional establishments such as doctor's offices, and lawyer's offices. They held signs bearing slogans that advised Germans to avoid Jewish businesses to protect their own interests. In some cases the SA attacked employees and caused damage to Jewish property; elsewhere, they simply provided an intimidating show of force. Some Jewish owned buildings were graffitied with anti Jewish slogans and yellow Stars of David.

Immediately following the day of the boycott, the Law for the Restoration of the Professional Civil Service was put into effect. This law removed Jews from every level of public office, by forcing them into retirement. Jews were no longer allowed to be university professors, school teachers, doctors, judges, or lawyers; and in the schools and universities, no more than 1% of the student body could be Jewish.

Jews who had served in the first World War were exempted from the ban between 1933 and 1934, but in 1935, during the Nuremberg Rallies, a new set of laws were announced which curtailed the rights of Jews further. The Nuremberg Laws stripped German Jews of their citizenship; there were no more special provisions for veterans. Non Jewish Germans were considered state citizens; German Jews were considered "state subjects".

Some scholars are of the opinion that during this period of the Nazi regime, the purpose of the anti Jewish measures was to encourage Jews to leave Germany and settle in other countries. Whether or not this is the case, in later years, after the Nazi government began arresting Jews and imprisoning them in concentration camps, emigration from Germany was made nearly impossible.

The year 1933 also saw the introduction of the first "racial hygiene" laws which targeted people with disabilities, or who were in any way deemed unfit to reproduce. The Law for the Prevention of Hereditarily Diseased Offspring mandated the forced sterilization of persons with learning disabilities, schizophrenia, bipolar disorder, epilepsy, Huntington's disease, alcoholism, or physical deformities, as well as those who had been born deaf or blind. Abortion, which had been illegal, was decriminalized in cases where the fetus was suspected of having any birth defects, though abortion of healthy "Aryan" fetuses was still against the law. Determinations as to who was subject to mandatory sterilization were made by Genetic Health Courts.

The practice of sterilizing the "unfit" was not unheard of elsewhere in the world. In the United States, for example, forced sterilization of persons in mental asylums was routinely carried out, and there were advocates for laws that would lead to practicing it on a larger scale. Catholics and others criticized German sterilization laws on religious grounds, but the Genetic Health Courts were admired for their clarity and well organized approach to "public hygiene" by others.

During this period, the first laws forbidding marriage and extramarital sexual relations between Jews and non Jews were passed.

Restriction of Women's Rights Under the Nazis

During the Weimar period, rights for women were substantially expanded from what they had been during the 19th century under the Imperial government. Not only were all women given the right to vote at the same age as men, but women were allowed to hold government positions, serve as representatives in the Reichstag, attend university, and become doctors, lawyers, and university professors, as well as participate in the sciences.

Under the Nazi regime from 1933 to 1939, women were still allowed to vote, but they were immediately excluded from political life, government professions, university posts, and prevented from practicing medicine and most areas of law. German girls were discouraged from attending university. The official Nazi organizations for women, most notably the

Jungmädel, for young girls and women, and the *NS-Frauenschaft*, for adult women, emphasized the centrality of marriage, motherhood, and housekeeping to women's lives. Young women were encouraged to be athletic and well educated, but not to be intellectuals or to pursue careers outside the home. A chief subject of young women's education was in how to avoid "racial defilement", or sexual relations with "non Aryans"; women who were caught in illicit sexual relations with Jews or other inferior races had their heads shaved, were paraded through town with signs around their necks declaring their crimes, and sometimes sent to concentration camps. German women who had more than four pure German children, on the other hand, were awarded the Golden Cross of the German Mother.

Nazi propaganda ostensibly claimed equality between the sexes, but underlined the separation of men's and women's spheres of responsibility. The few women who served in the Nazi government were generally excluded from upper level cabinet meetings and decision making. *Reichsführerin* Gertrud Scholtz-Klink, head of the *NS-Frauenschaft*, was the highest ranking woman in the Nazi government; she operated under the authority of the propaganda minister, Joseph Goebbels. Other prominent Nazi women included Leni Riefenstahl, the film director who created *Triumph of the Will*, Hitler's most famous propaganda film, and Hanna Reitsch, a pilot.

When World War II began in 1939, German women were permitted to join the German army; as in other countries, their roles were confined to administrative and logistical support staff, to free male soldiers for fighting on the front.

The Night of Long Knives
Hitler had risen to power on the backs of his Stormtroopers, or SA, the paramilitary organization which provided security at National Socialist party meetings in the 1920's, attacked their political opponents, and helped intimidate the Reichstag into voting for the Enabling Act of 1933.

The head of the SA was Ernst Rohm, a Nazi party member who had been with Hitler practically since the beginning of his career. Under Rohm's leadership, the SA was a serious rival to the power of the German army, the size of which had been capped at 100,000 soldiers by the Treaty of Versailles. Rohm's wish was to see the SA incorporated into the regular German army, a core unit at the heart of the German military. But by 1934, Hitler began to see the SA as a threat.

The SA operated primarily by intimidation through acts of street violence. They specialized in attacks such as those it carried out against Jewish businesses during the 1933 boycott. In the 1920's, when the Nazis were prone to brawling in the streets with the paramilitary units that protected rival political parties, the tactics employed by the SA had been useful, even essential. But once Hitler became Chancellor, he began to feel that his regime was above relying on an organization that many ordinary Germans perceived as being little better than gangsters. The SA were known to sometimes extort "protection" money from German businesses; the international reputation of the Nazis as "thugs" came from the uncontrolled bullying tactics employed by the SA.

Hitler wished to restore the glory of the official Germany army, who were natural rivals with the SA. He was also concerned by the fact that the SA, which constituted the left wing of the Nazi party, were virtually autonomous. Many SA members were socialists; that is to say, while their nationalistic fervor gave them common ground with Hitler, they were loyal to Rohm and to Germany, not to Hitler personally.

The final motivation for Hitler's split with the SA came in the form of a warning from President Paul von Hindenburg. While Hitler was the de facto leader of Germany, the President still had certain powers that Hitler could not match. Hindenburg was ill and nearing the end of his life in July of 1934, but he advised Hitler that the SA was a threat to German national security, and that if Hitler could not find a way to reign them in, Hindenburg would declare martial law. A military dictatorship would replace the Nazi government, and Hitler's Chancellorship would be stripped of power.

Hitler had a separate paramilitary organization that acted as his bodyguards, under the command of Heinrich Himmler, known as the *Schutzstaffel*, or SS, meaning "protection force." In June of 1934, Himmler claimed to have discovered evidence that the leaders of the SA, including Rohm, and conservative government members, such as Vice Chancellor Franz von Papen, were organizing a putsch to install a military dictatorship to replace Hitler. In the early hours of the morning on June 30th, SS forces, accompanied by the *Gestapo*, or Nazi secret police, dragged SA leaders from their bed and arrested them. In other major German cities, SA members were rounded up and shot. Over the next three days, as many as 1000 people were executed. The SA was obliterated, along with a number of

Hitler's former political allies who had helped him gain power.

Hitler Becomes Führer of Germany

President Paul von Hindenburg died of natural causes on August 2, 1934, less than a month after warning Hitler that he was considering the possibility of declaring martial law in Germany. Although it was Hindenburg who had named Hitler Chancellor of Germany in 1933, he and his conservative allies in the government had grown disillusioned with the Nazi regime. Hindenburg had only appointed Hitler as Chancellor in the first place because he believed that Hitler could be controlled. When this proved not to be the case, he and Vice Chancellor Franz von Papen began to discuss whether a constitutional monarchy could be reinstated. But it was too late for that; Hitler had consolidated his power based too carefully, and his control over the Reichstag was absolute. There was nothing the ailing Hindenburg could do except express his wishes for the restoration of the monarchy in his will, wishes which Hitler ignored.

After Hindenburg's death, Hitler, who up to this point had been careful to abide within the letter of the law and the Constitution in his bids for power, eliminated the office of the President of the Reich and combined it with the office of the Chancellor, thus making himself Germany's sole and supreme leader. During Hindenburg's state funeral, an army general by the name of Werner von Blomberg is supposed to have suggested that Hitler use the title of "Führer", or leader, which Hitler promptly adopted. In order to legitimize Hitler's position as supreme ruler of Germany, a national plebiscite, or vote, was held on August 19, 1934; 90% of the votes returned were in favor of Hitler. From this point, all persons in Germany swearing an oath of office were required to swear allegiance, in God's name, to Hitler personally, rather than to the government or to the country.

Rearmament of the Rhineland

In addition to imposing reparations on Germany, the Treaty of Versailles further sought to prevent

Germany from provoking another war by drastically restricting the size of its army. However, Germany had been rebuilding its military in secret even during the Weimar period, and once the Nazis took power, rearmament escalated. When President Paul von Hindenburg died in 1934, Hitler, now Führer of Germany, repudiated the Treaty of Versailles openly, and by 1935 German rearmament ceased to be clandestine.

One of the ways in which the Nazis had gained the support of the German people after the stock market crash of 1929 and the beginning of the Great Depression was by promising to revitalize the job market, a promise they proved able to keep. Unemployment practically came to an end during the Nazi period; rearmament efforts created enough jobs to keep all of Germany busy through the 1930's.

Under the Treaty of Versailles, Germany had surrendered certain territories to Allied forces, including Alsace-Lorraine, on the border between

Germany and France; the Treaty also stipulated that no German troops could be stationed in the Rhineland territory, on the border of Luxemborg, Belgium, and the Netherlands. In order to secure German compliance, French, American, Belgian, and British troops occupied parts of the Rhineland until 1935. The presence of black French Senegalese troops in this area excited intense racial anxieties on the part of the Nazi government. A small number of Rhineland women had married and had children with the black soldiers. The children of these unions were referred to as "Rhineland bastards" by the Nazis, and forced abortions of such mixed race children were mandated by the Genetic Health Courts.

In 1936, Hitler gave the order for the army to begin preparations for the German re-occupation of the Rhineland. There was some concern that France would attack the Rhineland in retaliation, but Hitler's order coincided with a change of government in France, and this distraction prevented a French armed response.

In later years, the lack of international opposition to Germany's re-militarizing the Rhineland was blamed for later, more aggressive moves made by the German army, such as the annexation of Austria and the invasion of Poland.

The Berlin Olympics of 1936

In 1931, prior to the Nazi takeover of Germany, the city of Berlin won the bid to host the 1936 Olympic games. Hitler saw the Olympics as an opportunity to improve the reputation of Nazi Germany abroad, as well as to demonstrate the validity of Nazi ideology regarding race—he believed that the "pure" German athletes would naturally dominate athletes of inferior races in every event.

As a result of the reputation that Germany had already gained abroad for its treatment of Jews, and its human rights record generally, the United States and several other European countries contemplated a boycott of the 1936 Olympics, particularly when

Hitler attempted to ban participation in the games by Jewish athletes. In response to the threatened boycott, Hitler agreed not to place restrictions on athletes based on ethnicity, and the boycott was abandoned.

In pursuit of this goal of masking the conditions German Jews were living under, the Nazi government made a quiet policy of relaxing the enforcement of anti Jewish laws in the weeks leading up to the Olympic games, as international tourists flooded Berlin. For instance, the infamous "Juden Verboten", or "Jews Forbidden" signs in the windows of businesses were removed before foreigners could see them. However, German athletes were given access to top rated sports training facilities and coaching, while Jewish athletes were scarcely permitted to set foot inside a gym.

Displeased by the withdrawal of the boycott against the Berlin games, African Americans in the United States made a special point of participating in the American delegation, sending twice the number of black athletes to Berlin that had competed in the 1932 Olympics in Los Angeles. Though African descended blacks in Germany were subject to intense persecution by the Nazi regime, special orders were given by Goebbels that American "Negroes" were to be treated on equal footing with all other American citizens.

While Germany won the greatest number of medals in the 1936 Olympic games, the individual athlete who took home the most gold medals was Jesse Owens, a black American from Ohio who competed in sprint and long jump events. Owens won four gold medals and broke three world records. Of the German athletes, only one "non Aryan" was permitted to compete: a half Jewish fencer named Helene Mayer, who won the silver. Six Hungarian Jewish athletes won gold medals in their events.

The 1936 Olympics in Berlin were considered a success by the Nazi regime. So pleased was Hitler with the outcome of the games that he reportedly wished for Germany to host them permanently. Foreign visitors returned home with glowing reports of their time in Germany. The measures taken to disguise the Nazi treatment of Jews had been successful. Only a few foreign journalists offered any resistance to Nazi propaganda in reporting on the Olympics in the newspapers.

Nazi Involvement in the Spanish Civil War

By the mid 1930's, Europe was increasingly divided between the democratic nations such as Britain and France, and the fascist regimes such as Italy, under Benito Mussolini, and Germany, under Adolf Hitler. (The sympathies of the Soviet Union, a dictatorship under Joseph Stalin, were still uncertain at this point.)

The ongoing European tensions between conservative Nationalist forces and left wing socialist Republican forces came to a head once again when civil war erupted in Spain in 1936. Hitler quickly dispatched Nazi planes to assist the Nationalist forces headed by General Francisco Franco, while the Soviet Union gave support to the Republican army. Hitler's reasons for assisting Franco were multilayered. First, a Nationalist government under Franco might prove to be an ally for Germany in the greater European conflict for which Hitler was already preparing. (This turned out not to be the case; Franco refused to bring Spain into the war, despite Hitler's repeated demands.) Second, Germany's participation in the Spanish civil war detracted attention from the extent of the rearmaments being carried out in Germany itself. Third, and perhaps most significantly, the Spanish conflict provided Germany with an opportunity to see how their aircraft and armored divisions performed in battle.

In addition to providing armaments to the Nationalist forces, the Nazis also provided training for their soldiers. As a direct result of German intervention, the Nationalist army under Franco defeated the Republican forces; Franco would govern Spain until 1975. German participation in the Spanish Civil War not only allowed the military to test the efficacy of its armaments, it provided boots on the ground combat training for young German officers who had never seen war before. Thus, participation in the Spanish Civil War played an important role in preparing the German army for the second World War. Historians consider the German army's preparedness to be chiefly responsible for Germany's devastating successes in the first three years of the second World War.

Anschluss

By 1938, the Nazi party had developed a significant presence in Austria, the country of Adolf Hitler's birth and Prussia's historical rival for power over the German territories. Discussions regarding Austria's merger with Germany had started just after the end of the first World War, begun by Social Democrats in Austria who were impressed by the new National Socialist government in Germany. But the merger had been forbidden under the terms of the Treaty of Versailles, which expressly disallowed any expansion of German territory.

The Austrian National Socialist party was in fact founded before the Nazi party in Germany, and is thought to have influenced its German counterpart in the early years of its development. The Austrian Nazi party pledged loyalty to Hitler beginning in the early 1930's, and Hitler commissioned a German Nazi lieutenant, Arthur Seyss-Inquart, to travel to Austria to influence the political situation in favor of annexation. In 1938, Austrian Chancellor Kurt von Schuschnigg was invited to visit Hitler at his summer home retreat in Germany, where Hitler attempted first to persuade, then to threaten him into inviting a German occupation of Austria. Schuschnigg countered with an offer to put the annexation question to a vote by referendum; reportedly, he was confident that Hitler's proposal would be defeated.

When Hitler threatened to stage a full scale invasion before the proposed referendum could take place, Schuschnigg resigned. Hitler and Schuschnigg both expected that the Austrian president, Wilhelm Miklas, would appoint Hitler's Nazi agent, Seyss-Inquart, as Chancellor in Schuschnigg's stead, but Miklas refused to do so. On the morning of March 12, 1938, when it had become apparent that the legitimate Austrian government would not be forthcoming with the invitation Hitler desired, Seyss-Inquart sent a telegram to Hitler, claiming that there were riots in Austria and formally requesting the help of the Germans to restore order. It was nonetheless obvious to countries such as Britain and France that the telegram was a pretext which Hitler had engineered. Once Nazi troops were installed in Austria, the referendum which Schuschnigg had proposed was carried out under Nazi supervision; Austrian Jews were barred from voting. Ninety nine percent of the votes were supposedly cast in favor of the annexation.

Political union between Germany and Austria had been Hitler's wish since the beginning of his political career; he made reference to it in *Mein Kampf*. The rest of Europe reacted, initially, with alarm—mostly because the *Anschluss* was in flagrant contempt of the

Treaty of Versailles. But France was in political turmoil for unrelated reasons, and Britain, under Neville Chamberlain, was reluctant to respond in a way that would be likely to provoke war. Most of the global community was uneasy about Hitler's obvious expansionist ambitions, but no European nation felt that it was prepared for another large scale conflict.

In the end, it was decided that Austria had the right of self-determination—that is, the right to decide for itself whether or not it wished to become a part of Germany. The fact that the Austrian people were not given the opportunity to vote on the matter in a free referendum was tacitly overlooked. High ranking Nazis, such as the German ambassador to Britain, Joachim von Ribbentrop, assured the international community that while Germany felt that it had right to reject the Treaty of Versailles and re-establish what he described as "sovereignty", it had no interest in encroaching on the sovereignty of any other nation. Rather, like the second German Empire under Bismarck, Germany would be content to be strong and inviolable while maintaining a peaceful and prosperous existence alongside its neighbors.

Later in 1938, however, Germany would set its sights on the Sudetenland, in Czechoslovakia.

The Munich Pact and the Annexation of the Sudetenland

The countries which we know today as the Czech Republic and Slovakia once formed the nation of Czechoslovakia, between 1918 and 1993. Czechoslovakia was formed after the first World War by the Treaty of St. Germain, as a union of territories and kingdoms which had belonged to the Austro-Hungarian empire. These territories were home to a number of different languages and ethnicities: more than half were Czech and Slovak, but over 20% were German. The area which was inhabited primarily by the German speaking residents of Czechoslovakia lay near the Sudetes mountains, along the north, west, and southwestern borders of the country. Referred to as the Sudetenland, this was amongst the wealthiest and best fortified areas of Czechoslovakia.

The expansion of German territory was forbidden by the Treaty of Versailles, but after the *Anschluss* of Austria it had become apparent that nothing short of war would make the Nazis consider the Treaty binding again. Neither Britain nor France felt prepared for another full scale conflict so soon after the last war, especially once Germany began to rebuild its navy, and Hitler did not wish to go to war with Britain and France if he could get what he wanted by diplomatic means. Therefore, in 1938, after Konrad Henlein of the Nazi-led Sudetenland Party had demanded and been refused independence by the government of Czechoslovakia, Hitler met privately to discuss the situation with British prime minister Neville Chamberlain at Hitler's summer home, Brechtesgarden—the same location where Hitler had met with the Austrian Chancellor, Kurt von Schuschnigg, to demand Austrian capitulation to the *Anschluss* plan.

Henlein and the Sudeten Nazis had for some time asserted that the German speaking peoples of Czechoslovakia were being unfairly discriminated against by the Czechoslovakian government, and because of this, the British and the French were concerned about the possibility of revolts and uprisings, which would justify military intervention by Germany. In September of 1938, representatives of the British, French, Italian, and German governments met in Germany, where they set down the terms of the Munich Pact, which effectively demanded that the government of Czechoslovakia allow the secession of the Sudetenland, since no support from Britain or France would be forthcoming if it chose to resist.

At Hitler's insistence, no representatives from the Czechoslovakian government were permitted to attend, and Britain agreed to these terms, which led to bitter resentment by the Czechoslovakian people against their supposed allies. Hitler claimed that, while Germany had a right to consolidate lands inhabited by ethnic Germans under a central German government, it had no desire to encroach upon the sovereignty of other nations. The British and the French chose to believe that Hitler's expansionism would be satisfied if his demands for the Sudetenland were met, and the people of Britain and France were relieved that war, which had seemed inevitable, had been averted. Britain and Germany signed a peace treaty the day after the Munich Agreement had been reached.

The actions of the British and French governments at this time constituted what is known as an appeasement policy, and it is viewed by historians as having emboldened Hitler to invade other countries in the upcoming years, as he was convinced that nothing would provoke the democratic powers to retaliate.

On October 1, 1938, the German army began its occupation of the Sudetenland. Because the Sudetes mountains had constituted Czechoslovakia's primary border defense, it was unable to prevent a full scale

German invasion in March of 1939.

Kristallnacht

One of the most notorious and frightening measures taken against German Jews by the Nazis in the years leading up to the war occurred on November 9th and 10th, 1938. You may remember that the date of November 9th was of great significance to the Nazis, being the date on which the republican government of Germany had been established in 1918, and the date of Hitler's failed "beer hall *putsch*" in 1923. On that date in 1938, members of the SS, the Gestapo, and the Hitler Youth attacked Jewish businesses, community centers, and synagogues, shattering so many windows that the event came to be known as *Kristallnacht*, the Night of Broken Glass, or *Reichspogromnacht*. (Pogroms were violent uprisings in 19th century Russia in which Jews in a particular area were attacked and killed, with the survivors driven out of the community.)

The events of *Kristallnacht* followed the sudden and

forcible deportation of around 15,000 Polish Jews from Nazi Germany in October of 1938. Herded into train cars and put off at the Polish border, they were denied entry into Poland and forced into refugee camps in the no man's land between Poland and Germany.

The parents of a seventeen year old boy named Hermann Grynszpan, who was living abroad in France at the time, were among the deportees. Grynszpan was angered by their treatment, and by the appeasement policies of France and Britain, which permitted Hitler to amass power and territory unchecked. On November 7, 1938, in what he declared to be an act of protest against Nazi persecution of the Jews, Grynszpan entered the German embassy in Paris and requested a meeting with the German ambassador, claiming to be a spy in possession of an important document. When told that the ambassador was out for the morning, he requested a meeting with the next most senior German diplomat. Grynszpan was granted an audience with an embassy official named Ernst vom Rath, who he shot five times. Rath died in a hospital two days later, on the 9th of November. Recent findings have suggested the possibility that Rath and Grynszpan had met previously and were lovers, and that this fueled Grynszpan's anger and sense of betrayal.

In the aftermath of *Kristallnacht*, the Nazi government maintained that the attacks against German Jews had not been organized by the state, but had rather been a spontaneous outpouring of anger over Rath's assassination. In reality, Joseph Goebbels, the Nazi propaganda minister, gave a speech shortly after Rath's funeral in the same Munich beer hall where the failed Nazi putsch had begun in 1923, in which he suggested that if the German people were to attack Jews, nothing would be done to stop them.

The *Kristallnacht* pogrom would not be confined to Germany; all Nazi controlled territories, including Austria and the Sudetenland, saw uprisings of violence against Jews on November 9, 1938.

Businesses were destroyed, synagogues were burned to the ground, and tens of thousands of Jewish men were arrested and shipped to concentration camps.

The following an excerpt of a memo, sent on November 9th, 1938, from Heinrich Müller, the Gestapo chief of operations, to all Gestapo offices:

"Actions against Jews, especially against their synagogues, will take place throughout the Reich shortly. [The memo is dated close to midnight.] They are not to be interfered with; however, liaison is to be effected with the Ordnungspolizei to ensure that looting and other significant excesses are suppressed [...]

Preparations are to be made for the arrest of about 20,000 to 30,000 Jews in the Reich. Above all well-to-do Jews are to be selected. Detailed instructions will follow in the course of this night."

Even before the outbreak of war in 1939, there was

widespread awareness in the foreign press of what Jews were enduring in the countries to which the Nazi regime had spread, but the European powers refused to intervene. Grynszpan's assassination of Rath was meant to bring foreign attention and pressure to bear on Nazi orchestrated Jewish persecution. While the assassination did not in itself succeed in doing this, the extraordinarily violent events of Kristallnacht did, to a certain extent: sympathy toward Germany abroad declined sharply, and the United States actually recalled its ambassador from Berlin.

The breakdown in relations with foreign governments did nothing to alter the treatment of Jews in Germany, however. Shortly after the Kristallnacht pogrom, Reynhard Heydrich, chief of the Gestapo, banned Jews from every aspect of public life: they were no longer permitted to be treated in hospitals, use public libraries, take public transportation, etc. Jews were forced to clean up the wreckage caused by the attacks, and all insurance claims for damages sustained during the pogrom were denied.

Chapter Six: The Third Reich At War

German Invasion of Poland

The Nazi invasion of Poland was the act which, after years of simmering tensions between the European powers, finally sparked the second World War.

Poland, like Czechoslovakia, had been created, or rather re-created, in 1919 by the Allies under the Treaty of Versailles. Poland had last existed as an independent state in the 18th century, only to be subsumed by Russia and Prussia in the 19th century. Prussian enmity against ethnic Poles, who strongly resisted "Germanization" during the century spent under Prussian rule, was severe; Bismarck had written that it was necessary to "crush" them.

In March of 1939, not long after forcing the Czechoslovakian government to cede the Sudetenland, Hitler's armies invaded all of Czechoslovakia—a move which Britain and France

had hoped to forestall, but which they were not
willing to take action to prevent. However, Britain
responded by guaranteeing the independence of
Poland, which, it was already known, had become an
object of interest to Germany. Chamberlain and Hitler
had signed a peace treaty between Britain and
Germany shortly after reaching the Munich
Agreement over the annexation of the Sudetenland,
but Germany's annexation of all Czechoslovakia
invalidated it, freeing Britain to stand behind Poland.
In other words, Britain made it known to Germany,
and to the rest of the world, that Poland was a line in
the sand: if Germany invaded, Britain, as well as
Poland's historical ally, France, would declare war.

However, after years of British and French
appeasement, Hitler was not convinced that either
nation would really prove willing to come to Poland's
defense. After all, Hitler's pretext for invasion was the
same one the democratic powers had accepted with
regards to Austria and the Sudetenland: the
unification of ethnic Germans under a central German

government.

In this case, the territory in question was the Free City of Danzig, the present day Polish city of Gdansk. The Free City of Danzig was an autonomous region, a port city on the edge of the Baltic Sea and the towns and villages that surrounded it. The population of Danzig was ethnically German and largely German speaking, and it had been part of Germany before the first World War. It was among the territories that Germany had been forced to cede by the Treaty of Versailles, though not to Poland, as Danzig was self-governing.

Danzig was, however, surrounded by Germany and Poland. It lay in a strip of land known as the Polish Corridor, which separated the principle mass of Germany from East Prussia, part of the historical Kingdom of Prussia. While the inhabitants of Danzig largely identified as German, only a small minority of people living in the Polish Corridor were German speaking. And yet, when Hitler laid claim to Danzig, he also insisted on the right to "liberate" the German minority in the Polish Corridor.

The first battle of World War II is held to have begun with the firing of German troops upon the Polish garrison in Danzig, but this action was only made possible by the Nazi-Soviet pact made in August of 1939. As we discussed in the previous chapter, the Soviet Union occupied a unique position among the world powers during this era: it was Communist, which made it anathema to the Nazis, but it was a dictatorship, which made it an uncomfortable ally for the western democracies. Yet the Soviet Union possessed the only army in the world large enough to seriously challenge the German Wehrmacht.

Stalin, fearful of Germany staging an invasion of Soviet territory via Poland, had attempted for most of the 1930's to establish a working alliance with Britain and France, and failed. As a result, when Hitler (who was nearly as wary of the Soviets as the Soviets were of Germans) sent his Foreign Minister into secret negotiations with the Soviet Foreign Minister, they were successful. The result was the Molotov-Ribbentrop Pact, a nonaggression agreement. This meant that if, for instance, Britain declared war on Germany, the Soviet Union would not make an alliance with Britain. The Pact also stipulated that Germany and the Soviet Union would have separate "spheres of interest"—in other words, Germany was free to invade and conquer as much of western Europe as it was able, and Russia would do the same in most of eastern Europe.

Hitler thought it unlikely that the British and the French would honor their commitment to go to war over Polish independence, but with the Ribbentrop-Molotov agreement under his belt, the possibility that they would honor it was less troubling. Germany also had the backing of the so called Pact of Steel, an alliance with Fascist Italy under Benito Mussolini; when Italy indicated that its armies were prepared for war, Hitler gave the order for the invasion of Poland on September 1, 1939. Britain and France issued an ultimatum, which Hitler ignored, and two days later, on September 3rd, both countries declared war on Germany. However, neither country's military forces were adequately prepared to halt the invasion, and after the Soviet army joined in, Poland was forced to surrender on September 27, 1939. Germany annexed the territories along its eastern border, including Danzig, Silesia, and the Polish Corridor (West Prussia) and installed a civilian puppet government over the remaining territory.

The "Phony War" and the Nazi Conquest of Western Europe

After the invasion of Poland and the declaration of war by Britain and France against Germany, there followed seven months during which little military action was carried out by other side, which resulted in the hostilities being deemed a "Phony War" in the European and American newspapers. Britain was too far away from Poland, geographically speaking, to launch an all out assault; such an action would have necessitated invading Germany outright, which their forces were not yet prepared to do. And in France and Britain both, there was a healthy fear of the German *Luftwaffe*, or air force, which was the strongest in the world. Both countries had seen the devastating effects of Nazi air attacks on Poland, destroying the railways and bringing transportation of goods and soldiers across the country to a halt.

It was believed by some that the lull in armed conflicts betokened a possibility of negotiating a new peace with Hitler, but these hopes were dashed in the spring of 1940, when Germany invaded Norway and Denmark. Norway was neutral at the beginning of the war, and Hitler was initially content in allowing it to remain so. But a former Norwegian defense minister and Nazi sympathizer, Vidkun Quisling, persuaded Hitler that a German invasion of Norway would be in the best interests of both countries. Norway was strategically important to both the Axis powers (the alliance consisting of Germany, Italy, and Japan) and the Allies (only Britain and France as of this point in the war) as the navies of both sides made use of its waters. But it was additionally important to Germany because its' near neighbor, Sweden, provided Germany with crucial supplies, such as iron ore. Denmark was invaded by Germany for the access it provided to the sea. The invasion of Denmark was only a matter of hours and constituted Germany's shortest armed action in the war.

With Scandinavia secure, in May of 1940 Germany turned its attention to France and the Low Countries—Belgium, Luxemborg, and the Netherlands. These invasions were conducted quickly, and the Low Countries, which were targeted first, were able to offer little resistance, despite the fact that warning of the invasion was sent to them by Hans Oster, a German officer who was working against the Nazi regime from the inside. With Belgium and Luxemborg under its control, Germany launched its invasion of France.

French defenses relied chiefly upon the Maginot Line—a line of concrete barriers along the French borders with Germany, Switzerland, and Luxemborg—to keep the Germans out. The Line had been built in the 1930's in order to secure the route the Germans had used to invade France during the first World War. To the north of the Maginot Line, however, lay the Ardennes Forest, a thickly wooded, hilly area which the French did not secure, in the belief that the German could not cross it. However, the German army had practiced an invasion scenario which accounted for the difficulty of traversing the Ardennes by rehearsing maneuvers in Germany's Black Forest, a similarly wooded terrain. Because the Allied forces were distracted by Germany's attack on Belgium, they were too scattered to mount an effective defense. The French forces, led by Charles de Gaulle, led a series of assaults against the German forces which were effective in the short term, but the majority of French forces were pinned behind the Maginot Line and could not meet the German advance. After the British Expeditionary Forces were cut off with no hope of assisting the French, they were withdrawn to Dunkirk—a move which some historians credit with saving 330,000 British and French troops from destruction.

The French forces fought alone, without substantial assistance from their allies, through June of 1940. The French government was forced to flee Paris on the 13th of June. German troops entered the city the next day, and on June 22, France surrendered. However, Free French forces which had escaped France before the occupation continued to fight abroad, and the French Resistance movement fought courageously within France against the Nazi Vichy government of Philippe Petain.

The Battle of Britain

"What General Weygand called the Battle of France is over. I expect that the Battle of Britain is about to begin. Upon this battle depends the survival of Christian civilization. Upon it depends our own British life, and the long continuity of our institutions and our Empire. The whole fury and might of the enemy must very soon be turned on us. Hitler knows that he will have to break us in this Island or lose the war. If we can stand up to him, all Europe may be free and the life of the world may move forward into broad, sunlit uplands. But if we fail, then the whole world, including the United States, including all that we have known and cared for, will sink into the abyss of a new Dark Age made more sinister, and perhaps more protracted, by the lights of perverted science."

Excerpt from a speech given by Winston Churchill to the House of Commons, June 18, 1940

Following the Nazi victory in France, Hitler set his sights upon Britain. Contemporary sources suggest that Hitler saw the invasion and conquest of Britain as the most important part of the Nazi plan for domination over western Europe. But the British navy and air force, as well as the geographical barrier posed by the English Channel, made a direct attack on Britain risky. In order to conquer Britain, Germany would have to first conquer its navy; and in order to destroy the navy, Germany fighter planes must have air supremacy. To achieve this, German fighters attempted to destroy English air bases.

Shortly after the fall of France to the Germans, Hitler made peace overtures to Britain. Despite the obstacle Britain posed to Germany's domination of Europe, Hitler admired Britain and saw its people as racially akin to Germans. But Britain had signed an agreement with France that neither country would seek a separate peace with Germany. Besides this, the prime minister with whom Hitler was accustomed to dealing was no longer in office, and the new prime minister, Winston Churchill, was not interested in peace with Germany.

The response of Germany was to bomb, then occupy, the Channel Islands belonging to Britain, and create an invasion plan for Britain called Operation Sea Lion, which was never carried out. Instead, in August of 1940, under an operation referred to as *Adler Tag*, or "day of the eagle", Germany began bombing British air bases along the coasts. The German air force, the *Luftwaffe*, was larger than the British air force, but the two countries possessed approximately the same number of fighter planes; the goal, therefore, was to destroy the British planes before they had a chance to get in the air. But the British had recently invented radar technology, which could detect the German planes and track their movements. German bombers suffered heavy losses as a result.

The Battle of Britain took a critical turn on August 24, 1940, when a German bomber mistakenly released its payload over Cripplegate, in London, destroying a church. The next day, the British bombed Berlin in retaliation; Hitler, outraged at the attack on Berlin, gave the orders which began the London Blitz.

The Blitz, or the German bombing of British cities (including London, Birmingham, Plymouth, Liverpool, Bristol, and Glasgow, as well as other cities) lasted from September 7, 1940, to May 21, 1941. London was attacked seventy one times, more than any other city; the bombs fell by day and night, while London residents went about their daily business as best they could, ready at the first sounding of the air ride sirens to hide in makeshift shelters, such as the London Underground. Those who could afford to do so moved to the countryside, away from the cities, or sent their children. Of the 40,000 civilians killed during the raids, half were Londoners.

The goal of the Blitz, from the German perspective, was to force a surrender by demoralizing the British population, while destroying wartime industries that supplied the British forces. But poor intelligence on the side of the Germans resulted in inefficient targeting of specific industries, and the damage they inflicted was, as a result, wide ranging but not devastating. Furthermore, the fact that the Nazi planes ceased bombing British air bases in order to bomb civilian targets has been credited with ensuring the survival of the British air forces.

The Battle of Britain is considered to be the Third Reich's first major defeat, and the beginning of the end of Hitler's dominance in Europe.

German Invasion of the Soviet Union

In May of 1941, Hitler brought an end to the London Blitz by moving his bombers to the east, in preparation for the invasion of the Soviet Union.

Though the Soviet Union had been an ally of Germany since the signing of the Molotov-Ribbentrop Pact of 1939, by 1941 Germany felt that the Communist nation had outlived its usefulness as a strategic partner. Hitler intended to dominate the entirety of eastern Europe, but in order to achieve this, he would first have to drive out the Soviet Union, Germany's only serious rival for power in that sector. The eventual destruction of the Soviet Union had been Hitler's intention since the beginning of his political career. He considered the "Slavic" peoples to be racially inferior to "Aryan" Germans. His goal, therefore, was to destroy the Soviet people, mine the country for its natural resources, and repopulate the country with Germans.

On June 22, 1941, Germany began Operation Barbarossa, the largest military operation of the second World War, extending along a front that was almost 3000 miles long. The targets were Leningrad, Moscow, and oil fields in the Caucasus. Initially, Germany's attacks against the Soviet Union was successful. Adopting the same blitzkrieg ("lightning war") tactics that had been used in the Battle of Britain, the German forces made rapid advances, with more than 150,000 Soviet casualties of the invasion reported after only the first week. German troops were expected to take control of Moscow by October.

The goal of the Nazi invasion of the Soviet Union was to eradicate Communism permanently. Prior to the invasion, secret Nazi agents were sent to the Soviet Union to assassinate key Jewish and Communist figures who might pose an ideological threat to Nazi dominance after the occupation had been accomplished. Nazi troops were carefully indoctrinated that the "Mongol hordes" they would fight in Soviet Russia were subhumans. For the Nazis, the war against the Soviet Union was both racial and ideological. The Nazis had been in a habit of conflating Communism and Jewishness since the party's earliest days; the propaganda that Nazi soldiers were steeped in was the old story in its most concentrated form.

Ironically, Joseph Stalin's reputation as a ferocious dictator who slaughtered his own people served as additional motivation for the German troops, who had been indoctrinated in the belief that National Socialism was not a dictatorship at all, but a people's movement. The invasion of the Soviet Union was intended as a war of annihilation, the utter destruction of not only its armies, but its civilian population the goal. Hitler believed that, as with the invasions of France and Poland, this would be accomplished within weeks.

However, the sheer size of the Soviet Russian army—nearly twice the size of the German army—as well as the determination of the Soviets to resist the Nazis, who had betrayed them, prevented the easy conquest Hitler had predicted. The Russian terrain, and the fact that the Germans were unprepared for ferocity of its winters, created severe obstacles. The Germans faced severe logistical difficulties in supplying their troops. By August of 1941, it had become clear that a quick victory in the Soviet Union was unattainable. In later years, scholars would attribute Nazi missteps in the Soviet campaign to Hitler's overconfidence after succeeding so rapidly in the conquest of France and Poland.

Despite the fact that the Germans were poised on the verge of seizing Moscow in the summer of 1942, Hitler decided that the German army should direct the main arm of its forces toward the invasion of Stalingrad (present day Volgograd), on the grounds that the defeat of Stalingrad would constitute a far more vicious blow against Soviet morale. But the Battle of Stalingrad, considered by some historians to be the largest battle in the history of warfare, proved to be the turning point of the war for Nazi Germany, and the beginning of its long defeat.

The Germans devastated the city with intense bombing throughout the summer; but by winter, their armies were surrounded by Soviet forces. Rather than retreating, the German forces attempted to hold the city, but they were cut off from their supply lines. In February of 1943, the German army in Stalingrad was forced to surrender. And because Hitler had ordered a postponement of the attack on Moscow until after Stalingrad was defeated, German forces lost the advantage which had been theirs during the summer.

When the weather turned, the German soldiers, who were not properly outfitted for a winter in Russia, began to take heavy losses. Frostbite, starvation, and the breakdown of tanks and trucks ground the German advance to a halt. Hitler had believed that the invasion would be over by the end of the summer, and had not prepared for the army's needs in cold weather. The Russian army obliterated German troops all along the 200 mile front; German losses amounted to a quarter of their army. Hitler reacted by dismissing dozens of members of his high command and taking control of the Germany army himself. Rather than withdrawing German forces in the Soviet Union, he ordered the army to hold the eastern front. Until the end of the war in 1945, German soldier held their place in Soviet Russia, fulfilling their orders to annihilate as much of the population as possible.

The Holocaust and the Final Solution

"The time is near when a machine will go into motion which is going to prepare a grave for the world's criminal—Judah—from which there will be no resurrection."

Quote from German newspaper *Der Stürmmer*,
January 1940

"It all happened so fast. The ghetto. The deportation. The sealed cattle car. The fiery altar upon which the history of our people and the future of mankind were meant to be sacrificed."

Elie Wiesel, Holocaust survivor, author of *Night*

In this chapter, we have examined the Third Reich as it waged war against most of Europe and the Soviet Union, from its early conquest of Poland and France to its defeat in the Battle of Britain and the pivotal moments in the invasion of Soviet Russia that marked the turning of the tide against Germany.

It is difficult to situate any study of the Holocaust into the timeline of the second World War, because it was comprised of events which happened incrementally, and were, with regards to the Final Solution, conducted in secret, even at the highest levels of the Nazi government. Furthermore, the Holocaust refers to the slaughter of the Jews by the Nazis on all fronts, including in the Soviet Union, where Einsatzgruppen followed in the wake of the German armies to destroy the Jewish populations of the areas occupied by the

Nazis.

But the Holocaust did not motivate any major conflicts during the war, because, in the sense that we understand it today, it was unknown outside the highest levels of the Nazi leadership. The Allies were largely unaware, and so were many Germans. The world at large knew that Jews living in the Third Reich were subject to persecution, but it was only after the concentration camps were liberated that the magnitude of what the Nazis had done began to be understood. For this reason, and for simplicity's sake, most timelines of the Holocaust begin with Hitler's appointment as Chancellor—since, after all, the persecution of German Jews began immediately after the Nazis took power.

We have covered such significant early events in the Holocaust as the opening of Dachau, the first concentration camp, in 1933; the Nuremberg Laws of 1935, which stripped Jews in the Third Reich of their citizenship; and Kristallnacht, the 1938 pogrom in which Jewish business and synagogues were destroyed, after which Jews were banned from any form of public life.

Starting in 1938, shortly before the beginning of the war, the Nazi government in Germany began to contemplate the "Final Solution to the Jewish Question"—in other words, how to rid the Third Reich of the Jewish population which remained in spite of years of persecution and pressure to leave Nazi controlled territories. Various schemes involving the forcible relocations of the Jews to places such as Madagascar, Tanganyika, and Palestine were discussed, but none came to fruition.

Many actions and small scale campaigns against Jews other than those we have discussed were carried out between 1933 and 1940, particularly once the war began and Hitler ceased to care about Germany's international reputation. After the invasion of Poland, which brought an additional 3 million Jews into the Third Reich, the brutality of Nazi persecution escalated sharply. All Jews living in Poland were rounded up into ghettos, concentrating their population in preparation for later slaughter. In 1941, the Jews of Austria were deported from their homes and forced into the same ghettos. The Krakow ghetto, containing 70,000 Jews, was sealed off from the rest of the city by a wall which Jewish inhabitants were forced to construct themselves.

Heinrich Himmler, chief of the SS and principle architect of the Final Solution, ordered the expansion of Auschwitz and the construction of a camp at Birkenau in 1941, in preparation for later events. By 1942, when the concentration camps were outfitted with gas chambers and thus converted into death camps, over a million Jews had been murdered already.

While Hitler had ordered Himmler to begin putting together a plan for Jewish genocide in 1938, it was only after the invasion of the Soviet Union began to go wrong, and after the entry of the United States into the war in December of 1941, that Hitler made the decision to begin the extermination during the war, rather than after. The Final Solution—the plan to exterminate the Jews by transporting them to concentration camps and executing them en masse—was created at the Wannsee Conference, a meeting of senior Nazi officials, in late January 1942. This was a meeting to arrange cooperation in the plan between the various government agencies, rather than a debate on whether to implement the order.

An early proposed method of killing the Jews was by transporting them in forced labor units to eastern Europe, where they would be worked to death building roads; anyone strong enough to survive the work would be shot. But as the war in the Soviet Union dragged on, the logistical difficulties of transporting Jewish prisoners to the front defeated the project. Himmler himself, somewhat famously, attended the execution by firing squad of 200 Jews in Belarus, and the sight disturbed him to such a degree that he became physically ill. He determined that if firing squads became the primary tool of the genocide, the morale of German soldiers would break down entirely. Gas chambers, it was decided, would be more efficient for murdering large numbers of Jews at once, as well as more humane—not to the Jews who were being murdered, but to the German soldiers who were murdering them.

This feeling of Himmler's—that the murder of Jews on such a vast scale would horrify anyone, no matter how ardent a Nazi and Jew hater they might be—is probably responsible for the secrecy and use of euphemisms surrounding the Final Solution. References are made in the memos and paperwork generated at the Wannsee Conference to the "evacuation east" of the Jews, but it was understood by all present that this was code for murder. Where the German public was concerned, the pretense that Jews were being "evacuated" for labor was maintained until the end of the war.

Below, an extract from one of the notorious "Posen

speeches" made by Himmler in October of 1943 contains the first open and undisguised acknowledgements ever made by a Nazi official regarding the intentional slaughter of the Jews. It also refers to the deliberate secrecy around the subject.

"I ask of you that that which I say to you in this circle be really only heard and not ever discussed. We were faced with the question: what about the women and children? I decided to find a clear solution to this problem too. I did not consider myself justified to exterminate the men—in other words, to kill them or have them killed and allow the avengers of our sons and grandsons in the form of their children to grow up. The difficult decision had to be made to have this people disappear from the earth. For the organization which had to execute this task, it was the most difficult which we had ever had. [...] I felt obliged to [...] speak about this question quite openly and to say how it has been. The Jewish question in the countries that we occupy will be solved by the end of this year. Only remainders of odd Jews that managed to find hiding places will be left over."

Historian Raul Hilberg breaks the implementation of the Final Solution down into a series of measures. First, the Nazis decided who was Jewish. Definitions of Jewishness were based on race rather than religion. According to the Simon Wiesenthal Center, the Nazis defined a Jew as:

"Anyone with three Jewish grandparents; someone with two Jewish grandparents who belonged to the Jewish community on September 15, 1935, or joined thereafter; was married to a Jew or Jewess on September 15, 1935, or married one thereafter; was the offspring of a marriage or extramarital liaison with a Jew on or after September 15, 1935."

Jews who met these guidelines were required to register. In 1938, Jews were required for new identification papers which were stamped with J's, and any Jew not possessing an obviously Jewish name were required to add "Sarah" or "Israel" to their names, for easy identification. By September of 1941, Jews were required to wear the infamous Star of David badge when in public.

The next step was the systematic stripping of property, businesses, gold and silver, land, works of art, and other valuables from the Jews. Property registration was also required starting in 1938. Emigration of Jews from Germany skyrocketed during that year, and via the process of "Aryanization", property and funds were stripped from all Jews as they attempted to flee the country. Of the 500,000 Jews living in Germany in the 1930's, about 300,000 managed to flee before emigration was halted.

Ghettoization, or forcing Jewish populations to concentrate in certain areas of the cities, was the next step, which eased the way to the final one: rounding them up and transporting them to the death camps.

There is a great deal of debate amongst historians as to whether or not Hitler ever gave a direct order to murder every Jew in Europe, or whether the effect was achieved indirectly. The indoctrination and ideological uniformity required of all Nazis more or less assured that the destruction of the Jewish race was an outcome which everyone claimed to desire, but it had to be achieved by direct action. This ambiguity has given rise to a phenomenon of Holocaust denial—an unscholarly fringe belief, propagated by modern neo-Nazis and white supremacists, that the murder of over half the Jews in Europe was merely a coincidental outcome of the general destruction of the second World War. But whether Hitler gave the order and ordered the records destroyed, or whether he made his desires known indirectly to his loyal lieutenants whose purpose was to make his will manifest, the Holocaust is undeniable to anyone with a passing familiarity with the historical record.

Between September and October of 1941, the sites of

new concentration camps were selected, the methods by which the Jews could be killed in large numbers were tested and finalized, Jewish emigration from the Third Reich was forbidden, and the first groups of Jews were transported toward the camps.

One of the decisions made at the Wannsee Conference was to forestall accusations of cruelty against the Nazi government by creating a concentration camp specifically for Jews over 65 years old, as well as those who had been wounded or received the Iron Cross in the first World War. Thereseinstadt camp was jokingly referred to by Nazi high command as a spa resort where elderly Jews could retire in peace. In reality, it was a place to stow Jews who were not able bodied, and whose feeble appearance would damage the plausibility of the "evacuation east for labor" story. Thereseinstadt was also the camp to which Mischlings, or half and quarter Jews were sent.

Historian draw a distinction between the majority of

the concentration camps, where prisoners were killed by being worked to death under miserable conditions, and the death camps, which were outfitted with gas chambers and used primarily for mass murder. Prisoners who were sent to the death camps only survived for a matter of hours after their arrival on the trains. Such concentration camps as Ravensbruck, Buchenwald, and Bergen-Belsen—what one senior Nazi official official referred to during the Nuremberg Trials as the "normal" camps—were built in Germany before the start of the war to hold undesirables, such as homosexuals and Rom people as well as Jews. This was in contrast with the six death camps, which, for secrecy, were built outside of Germany, mostly in Poland: Chelmno, Belzec, Sobibor, Treblinka, Auschwitz, and Trostenets. (Some historians also include Majdanek.) Even in the "normal" camps, the mortality rate of prisoners was 75%. Auschwitz alone gassed approximately 6,000 Jews a day and was responsible for the deaths of over one million Jews by the time the camp was liberated in 1944.

Approximately 2,700,000 Jews were killed in the death camps. More than six million died in the Holocaust altogether. News of the planned annihilation reached the American president of the World Jewish Congress in 1942, who made it public. Ten nations, including the US and Britain, declared their intention to prosecute German soldiers for war crimes. This is thought to be part of the reason why so many documents surrounding the Final Solution and the Holocaust were destroyed before the end of the war, as senior Nazis saw their impending defeat, and sought to eliminate incriminating evidence against them.

Chapter Seven: Downfall of the Third Reich

Germany Declares War on the United States

On December 7, 1941, Germany's ally, Japan, attacked a U.S. naval base in Hawaii called Pearl Harbor. The United States retaliated with an immediate declaration of war against Japan. A few days later, Germany declared on war on the United States. Historians are unsure precisely why Hitler chose to do this, since the terms of Germany's alliance with Japan did not require it. Some have theorized that Hitler, excited and admiring of the Japanese sneak attack, was simply acting erratically. Others point to the fact that the U.S. had been giving supplies to Britain on credit under the Lend-Lease act for several years, and a formal declaration of war allowed Germany to attack American ships in the Atlantic with U-boats (submarines). Nazi racial policy may also have played a role: Hitler saw the United States as a corrupt and racially impure society that stood little chance of victory against "Aryan" troops.

While all of these factors must have influenced Hitler's decision, along with the fact that he wished to divert attention from the fact that the invasion of the Soviet Union had permanently stalled after a successful summer campaign, the declaration of war was welcome news to American president Franklin Roosevelt, who had long wished to take action against Nazi Germany. Since the beginning of the Great Depression, which brought an end to such international cooperation schemes as the Young plan, the United States had been ardently isolationist with regards to the conflict in Europe. Since the German occupation of France, however, Roosevelt had been painfully aware that Britain, America's oldest ally, was the last democracy withstanding fascism on the European continent. He saw the spread of Nazism as a threat to American freedom, but was unable to gain the support he needed to declare war on Germany until Germany had first declared war on the United

States.

At the time, the United States was one of the wealthiest countries in the world, but it was not a dominant military power. This, no doubt, was another reason Hitler did not hesitate to declare war. Despite the fact that the U.S. had first been attacked by Japan, American dedicated 90% of its wartime resources towards the destruction of the Nazi forces.

Nazi Defeats in German North Africa and the Invasion of Italy

Early American efforts in the war focused on fighting the Germans and Italians in North Africa. From November 8 to November 11, 1942, American and British coalition forces under General Dwight D. Eisenhower carried out Operation Torch in Algeria and Morocco, French colonies which had come under Nazi control after the fall of France.

The African conflicts were of vital importance to the

war; Britain was a controlling power in Egypt, and the Germans were intent on gaining control of the Suez Canal and blocking Allied access to Middle Eastern oil reserves. Besides Operation Torch, the conflict in Africa also stretched into Egypt, Libya, and Tunisia.

The Axis forces were hard hit during the North African campaigns. German and Italian casualties were triple those of the American and British forces. By the end of November of 1942, the Allies had crossed the Tunisian border in the northwest, which enabled them to invade Sicily by summer of 1943, and from there, the Italian mainland.

Benito Mussolini was the Fascist dictator of Italy. In the 1920's and 1930's, the Nazis had greatly admired the Italian Fascists, modeling their look and ideology on Mussolini's "Blackshirts". However, once Italy entered into the Tripartite Alliance with Germany, it became almost entirely subordinate to Germany. By the time the Allies invaded Sicily, opposition groups in Italy, disillusioned with Mussolini, were engaged in overthrowing his government.

After Mussolini was arrested on September 3, 1943, the new government began negotiating surrender with Eisenhower, who agreed that as long as the Italians assisted the Allies in forcing the Germans from Italy, they would be treated leniently. However, the British and Americans lost Rome to German forces in 1944, and were unable to retake it right away, as preparations were underway for D-Day. Ultimately, German forces in Italy did not surrender until a few days before Germany was defeated in April of 1945.

D-Day Invasion

In 1941, after Germany invaded the Soviet Union, thus breaking the alliance between the two countries forged in the Molotov-Ribbentrop Pact, Stalin began negotiations to enter into an alliance with the British. Because Churchill was not willing to agree to Stalin's demands for territory, the negotiations dragged on until 1942, at which point Stalin conceded his territorial demands. Stalin began to press the Allies for reinforcements along the western front, but Churchill informed him that the Allies were not yet prepared for an invasion of this magnitude, and would be concentrating their efforts in Africa for the time being.

For three days in November and December of 1943, at a conference in Tehran, the "Big Three" leaders—Churchill, Roosevelt, and Stalin—met in person for the first time. Since 1941 they had been negotiating cooperation via telegrams and through diplomatic channels regarding where to deploy American forces. Stalin, whose Soviet army had inflicted the bulk of German casualties since the beginning of the invasion, was eager for the United States and Britain to invade occupied western Europe. Such an action would create the two-front war Hitler had been trying to avoid since the beginning and take pressure off Soviet forces in the east. Additionally, while Stalin was no longer asking for the exact same disposition of territory that he had brokered with Hitler, he demanded that eastern Europe be left under Soviet control after the war, and the borders of Poland be redrawn in the west. In exchange for this, Stalin agreed that the Soviet army would make a push to Germany from the east.

Plans for Operation Overlord, codename for the invasion of Normandy, were drawn up as a consequence. Over the course of the following year, immense preparations were made for British and American troops to cross the English Channel and liberate France from German occupation. The British had attempted an invasion of this kind at Dieppe in 1941, but it had not been successful. The chief difficulty lay in the fact that the Germans were well aware that an Allied invasion attempt from across the Channel was to be expected, and they had put enormous effort into fortifying the French coast in this area so as to repel it.

Under the direction of Field Marshal Erwin Rommel, who had been the commander of German forces in

North Africa, Rommel constructed a fortification known as the Atlantic Wall: miles and miles of concrete fortifications, not unlike the Maginot Line, which would make a landing from the sea impossible. The Germans were aware that the invasion would take place in 1944, and that the Wall would not be completed in time, so the beaches where the Wall did not reach were filled with barbed wire and more than a million land mines. In the waters off the beaches, Rommel sank constructions of jagged debris which would tear holes into the hulls of any ships that attempted to approach.

On the American side, Eisenhower, and General Bernard Montgomery were in charge of the Allied troops. New technologies were developed to help bypass the German defenses: the British created Mulberry harbors, which were portable, floating docks that facilitated the off-loading of cargo from ships into floating pallets that could be brought to shore without the ships having to approach too nearly. Royal engineers under General Percy Hobarth were also responsible for the design of "Hobart's funnies", tanks which had been designed to compensate for the difficulties encountered during the failed invasion of Dieppe. The presence of these tanks made it possible for the Allied troops to push through the German defenses once they were on the ground.

In the early morning of D-Day, June 6, 1944, American, British, and Canadian troops landed on the beaches along the French coast. The beaches each had code names: the British landed on Gold and Sword Beaches; the Canadians on Juno Beach; and the Americans on Utah and Omaha Beaches. The American landing at Omaha Beach has become the most famous in the decades since the war ended because the German forces were strongest there and the Americans suffered the greatest casualties as a consequence.

German response to the Normandy invasion was delayed by initial confusion as to whether it was a diversion to draw attention from a "real" invasion further north in Calais, and by the fact that Rommel was a four hour drive from away from the battle and thus unable to give orders. Rommel, and the Nazi high command, had been expecting the invasion to land at Calais, because the Channel crossing is narrowest there. The Allies encouraged this idea through Operation Bodyguard, a decoy mission which planted false intelligence for German interception pointing towards the Calais invasion. When told that the Allies had landed in Normandy, Hitler denied his commanders permission to bring in reinforcement for hours because he was so convinced there would be an invasion at Calais.

On the first day of the Allied invasion of Normandy, 150,000 British, American, and Canadian troops landed on the coast and began a push toward Paris. A week later, there were 500,000. On August 25, 1944, after taking more than 75,000 Germans prisoners, the Allies arrived in Paris, where the commander of the German garrison surrendered.

The July 20th Plot

When Hitler took command of the army, after the invasion of the Soviet Union began to stall in the winter of 1943, his general staff were forced to acknowledge that his decision making had grown erratic. Hitler was fanatically committed to his vision of the Third Reich as a glorious, racially pure empire. The alternative to him was worse than death. If the Third Reich was to fail, Hitler seemed to feel that it would be best for every man, woman, and child in Germany to die fighting its enemies—and for every home, building, road, and railway in Germany to be destroyed in the battle. Hitler's military staff knew that his two-front war against the Soviet Union and the Allied invasion of occupied France was suicidal, and that if Germany did not surrender, the entire country would soon be destroyed. But he would not listen to any suggestion of making peace with the Allies or withdrawing German forces from the front.

Long before 1944, a number of conspiracies against Hitler—whether to arrest and put him on trial or to assassinate him—had been attempted over the years and come to nothing. In fact, the conspirators involved in the most famous assassination plot, known as Operation Valkyrie, or the July 20th plot, tried to kill Hitler at least four times before they were caught and executed. Hitler was paranoid, surrounded by loyal guards, and rarely appeared in public. Opportunities for assassination were limited.

On July 20, 1944, a young officer by the name of Claus von Stauffenberg, who was chief of staff for a member of Hitler's general staff, planted a briefcase containing a bomb beneath the table where Hitler was sitting, then left the room. Had the bomb detonated where it was placed, Hitler would certainly have died, but one of his staffers moved it aside at the last moment because it happened to be in his way. Believing the assassination had been successful, Stauffenberg and the other conspirators activated their plan to assume control of the reserve army. When word came down that Hitler had survived the bombing, Stauffenberg and his compatriots were arrested by a fellow conspirator hoping to save himself from exposure. The July 20th conspirators were executed by firing squad the next day, except for Field Marshal Erwin Rommel, who was famous and well liked; he agreed to commit suicide to save his family.

Hitler, incensed by the fact that the conspiracy had originated within his own general staff, sent the SS on a punitive rampage fueled by paranoia. Seven thousand people were arrested, and five thousand were executed. This included anyone who could be remotely construed as being connected with the plot, all the families of the conspirators and those suspected of being connected to the conspiracy, and a number of people whom it was convenient for the SS to dispose of for unrelated reasons.

The Battle of Berlin and Hitler's Final Days

By the spring of 1945, the Third Reich was in utter disarray. Two divisions of the Soviet army were racing each other to capture Berlin, attacking from the east and the south, while a third captured a German military base defending Berlin to the north. In 1944, Soviet forces had begun to march through Poland, where they began liberating the concentration camps, including Auschwitz, though not before camp guards attempted to hide their crimes by evacuating prisoners on forced death marches. The armies now bearing down on the center of Germany vastly outnumbered the remaining army in terms of both men and equipment. The rapidity of the Soviet reproach was reportedly due to the fact that Stalin was frantic to reach Berlin before the Allies did.

American, British, and Canadian forces were advancing on Berlin from a newly freed France. Between April 8 and April 29, six concentration camps were liberated: Buchenwald, Bergen-Belsen, Sachsenhausen, Flossenburg, and Dachau. Germany no longer had control of Belgium, Luxemborg, or the Netherlands. Hitler had conquered all of western Europe more swiftly than anyone had thought possible, but the disastrous campaign in the Soviet

Union and the two front war had stretched his armies too thin, and total defeat was imminent. Accounts of the Nazi regime's last few months suggest that everyone knew the end had come, even Hitler; but Hitler was determined that Germany would resist to the last person.

The Nazi regime was in such dire peril that by January of 1945 Hitler had taken up permanent residence in his secret underground bunker, along with his companion, Eva Braun, and top members of his staff and their families, including Joseph and Magda Goebbels and their six children.

Hitler's 56th birthday, April 20, 1945, was the first day the advancing Soviet artillery fire began to fall on Berlin. It was also the last day that Hitler set foot outside the shelter of the Führerbunker. Despite the urgings of his general staff to flee Berlin, Hitler was determined to remain and take charge of the city's defenses. A large number of those fighting to defend Berlin—some 45,000—were children, elderly, or disabled. On April 20th, Hitler awarded the Iron Cross, Germany's highest military honor, to child soldiers of the Hitler Youth. These boys, some of whom were as young as ten, were manning portable anti-tank guns to fire on Soviet tanks, which made for slow and clumsy targets as they navigated the city streets over obstacles and bombing rubble.

Many of Hitler's staff fled Berlin as the Soviets advanced, including Heinrich Himmler, head of the SS. Over the course of the war, Hitler had repeatedly come into conflict with the conservative military elite of the old school, who were guided more by the ethics of "honorable" warfare than by Nazi ideology; these officers had no stomach for the slaughter of women, children, and civilians. When asked for permission to evacuate the two million civilians remaining in the city, Hitler only reiterated that every citizen of the Reich had a duty to die in its defense.

The German 12th army under General Felix Steiner had withdrawn from the western front—the battles being fought against the Allies in Europe—and was thus available for the defense of Berlin. Hitler ordered the 12th army to attack the Soviet army in conjunction with the German 9th army, which would attack from the opposite side in a pincer movement. But unbeknownst to Hitler, several divisions of the 12th army had been deployed elsewhere, and what remained of Steiner's troops were outnumbered by the Soviets ten to one. Lacking the necessary numbers to make an attack anything more than a suicide gesture, Steiner refused the order. When news of his refusal was relayed to Hitler on April 22nd, it triggered an emotional meltdown and accusations of treachery against his generals. He declared that the war was lost, that everyone could do as they liked, and that he would commit suicide in the near future.

By April 27, 1945, Berlin was entirely cut off by the Allied forces, and there was little left for the inhabitants of the city to do except await death or capture. The invading Soviet army had earned a terrifying reputation for rape and indiscriminate murder of civilians, partly in retribution for the atrocities committed by the Germans during their invasion of the Soviet Union. On April 28, Hitler received word that Himmler had attempted to convince the Allies that he had the authority to negotiate the surrender of Germany; Hitler interpreted this as a betrayal, and executed Himmler's SS representative in the bunker. He had already ordered the arrest of Hermann Goring, for a similar attempt at usurping power.

Later that day—just after midnight on April 29—Hitler and Eva Braun were married in a civil ceremony. The Soviet army had reached Potsdam, and had seized the Chancellery building; there was no longer a remote possibility of escape. That same day, Hitler discovered that Mussolini and his mistress had been murdered and their bodies defiled in a ditch. Having already consulted with his personal doctor as to the best method of committing suicide, Hitler dictated his will to his private secretary. The next day, April 30, 1945, as the Soviet army lay within 1600 feet of the Führerbunker, Hitler and Eva Braun said goodbye to their staff, retreated to Hitler's private study, and committed suicide: Braun, by cyanide, and Hitler by a combination of cyanide and a gunshot to the head. According to Hitler's instructions, their bodies were taken into the garden and burned. Many others in the bunker committed suicide as well, including Joseph Goebbels, his wife Magda, and their children, all six of whom were under the age of twelve.

On May 8, 1945, Hitler's appointed successor, Admiral Karl Dönitz, authorized the unconditional surrender of German forces to General Eisenhower of the Allies. The second World War would continue another few months, as Allied forces continued to fight Japan in the Pacific theater, but the Third Reich was finished forever.

Epilogue

In this book we have attempted to give you an overview of the Third Reich and the political, economic, and societal context which gave rise to the Nazi party. In so doing, we have made a brief sketch of the history of the Holy Roman Empire, gone into some detail about the unification of Germany under Otto von Bismarck, and outlined the state of Germany after the first World War and during the Weimar Republic, before sketching the birth of Nazism, the effects of the Nazi regime on Germany, and Nazi Germany's participation in World War II.

So far, our task has been relatively simple; the historical record speaks for itself. However, any sort of afterword is difficult. The impact of the Third Reich and Nazism upon the historical and political landscape of the 20th century has been immeasurable, defying neat summation.

Our goal in placing the rise of Nazism into its historical context has been demystification. Everyone knows, or thinks they know, the basics about Nazi Germany, from high school, from films, and from pop culture. Yet without some deeper study, it is difficult to separate the reality of Nazism from the caricatures that are embedded in the popular consciousness: shouty men in uniforms, marching in lockstep, mindlessly saluting their Führer. Nazism has become a cultural shorthand for evil, for totalitarian governments, for racism and genocide. As a result, it is difficult for us to see the Nazis as humans. We cannot imagine having anything in common with a Nazi. Probably we all like to believe that if we had been living in Germany in the 1920's and 1930's, we would have been immune to the Nazi allure; even if we are not Jewish, gay, Rom, Jehovah's Witnesses, or Communists, we like to think that we would have resisted, even at the cost of our lives. We believe that we would have seen the swastikas and immediately drawn the connection to the torture and murder of millions of people, the gas chambers and crematoriums, the tanks and the bombs.

Of course, many ordinary Germans did resist the Nazis, either openly or through subterfuge. But the Nazis gained power, ultimately, through democratic elections. And while those who had voted them into power were not necessarily prepared for all the consequences that resulted, the Nazis never made any secret of their beliefs and agendas. Few Nazi supporters were confirmed haters of Jews until the Nazis told them that the Jews were responsible for the devastation of Germany. And would anyone have cared what the Nazis believed about Jews if they were not already attracted to the Nazi vision of a strong, prosperous, dominant German empire?

The great danger in reducing the Third Reich to a cartoon, or a realm of fairytale monsters without human qualities, is that it takes us off our guard; we cease to see the patterns when they are reproduced in our own societies. Nationalists and neo-fascists today generally know that they will not be taken seriously if they make anti-Semitic remarks in public; the legacy of Hitler has made use particularly sensitive to anti Jewish bigotry (though it has by no means vanished from Western culture.) But when the same racist rhetoric is applied to Muslims, to immigrants, to refugees, do we always see the resemblance between our own prejudices and those exploited by the Nazis?

Hannah Arendt, a 20th century Jewish philosopher and Holocaust survivor, writes about the necessity of skepticism and doubt in the face of totalitarianism. Germany after World War I was a country in crisis, and in any time of national crisis, when people seek the reassurance of strong leaders who appear to have all the answers, doubters and skeptics tend to be treated as disloyal and dangerous. But it was the unthinking, unquestioning belief of Hitler's followers that made him powerful; the ruthlessness with which the Nazis suppressed dissent only solidified his control.

Adolf Hitler, Joseph Goebbels, Heinrich Himmler,

and every Nazi party member who collaborated in the genocide of six million Jews, were human beings much like ourselves. Hitler was extremely fond of dogs and children. His personal secretary described him as a kind and fatherly employer. Hitler and Goebbels often discussed policy with Goebbel's six children playing underfoot. They all saw themselves as building something beautiful for themselves and generations of Germans to come. And they were not immune to the horror of their own actions; the secrecy and euphemisms which surrounded the implementation of the Final Solution testifies to this.

This excerpt from one of Himmler's Posen speeches goes a little way towards illustrating the thoughts of a man who recognizes that what he is doing is inhumane, but is nonetheless committed to carrying it out in the service of a "higher cause":

"One principle must be absolute for the SS man: we must be honest, decent, loyal and friendly to members of our blood and to no one else. What happens to the Russians, what happens to the Czechs, is a matter of utter indifference to me. Such good blood of our own kind as there may be among the nations we shall acquire for ourselves, if necessary by taking away the children and bringing them up among us."

It is useless to pretend for our own comfort that the Nazis were not like us, or that all of the Nazis, including Hitler himself, were not capable of warmth, kindness, compassion, and generosity. But it is easy to see where monstrousness established its foothold: it was in the drawing of a line between themselves and people they saw as not like themselves. The protection of human identity was bestowed only on a few. Everyone else, they categorized as *untermenschen*, sub-human; and what happened to sub-humans, as Himmler says, was a matter of utter indifference.

The Nazis did not invent the practice of distinguishing between one group of people that were entitled to human identity and others that weren't; they inherited those ideas from the generations that came before them. Their ancestors were also our ancestors. Some of the same prejudices exist in our modern way of thinking. Let us never fail to question them, or to remain doubtful and skeptical when those in power capitalize on our fears of the differences between us and those we perceive as different.

References and Further Reading

Arendt, Hannah. *Eichmann in Jerusalem: A Report On the Banality of Evil*. London: Penguin, 1976.

Maschmann, Melita. *Account Rendered: A Dossier On My Former Self*. Abelard-Schuman,1965.

Hildebrand, Klaus. *Das Dritte Reich*. Vol. 17. Oldenbourg Verlag, 2009.

Himmler, Heinrich. "The Complete Text of the Poznan Speech." (1943).

Hitler, Adolf. *Mein Kampf*. Trans. Ralph Manheim. Boston: Houghton Mifflin 305 (1971): 325-327.

Shirer, William L. *The Rise and Fall of the Third Reich*. Simon & Schuster, New York 37 (1960): 1938-1943.

United States Holocaust Memorial Museum. http://www.ushmm.org. Accessed December 15, 2015.

CPSIA information can be obtained
at www.ICGtesting.com
Printed in the USA
LVHW012104210922
728942LV00003B/406